# SHORT WALKS FROM
## ——PUBS IN——
### *Exmoor and North Devon*

*Other areas covered in the Pub Walks series include:*

Bedfordshire
Berkshire
Birmingham & Coventry
Bournemouth & Poole
Bristol & Bath
Buckinghamshire
Cambridgeshire
Cheshire
Chilterns
Cotswolds
Cotswold Way
County Durham
North & West Cumbria
South Cumbria
Dartmoor & South Devon
Derbyshire
Essex
West Essex
Gloucestershire
Herefordshire
Hertfordshire
Icknield Way Path
Isle of Wight
Kent
Lancashire
Leicestershire & Rutland

Lincolnshire
North London
Middlesex & West London
Midshires Way
Norfolk
Northamptonshire
Nottinghamshire
Oxfordshire
Shropshire
South Downs
Staffordshire
Suffolk
Surrey
Surrey Hills
Thames Valley
North Wales
South Wales
Warwickshire
Wayfarer's Walk
Wiltshire
Worcestershire
Wye Valley & Forest of Dean
East Yorkshire
North Yorkshire
South Yorkshire
West Yorkshire

*A complete catalogue is available from the publisher at*
*3 Catherine Road, Newbury, Berkshire.*

# SHORT WALKS FROM —————PUBS IN—————
## *Exmoor and North Devon*

Charles Whynne-Hammond

COUNTRYSIDE BOOKS
NEWBURY, BERKSHIRE

COUNTRYSIDE BOOKS
3 Catherine Road
Newbury, Berkshire

ISBN 1 85306 402 5

Designed by Mon Mohan
Cover illustration by Colin Doggett
Photographs by the author
Maps by Glenys Jones

Produced through MRM Associates Ltd., Reading
Printed by J W Arrowsmith Ltd., Bristol.

# Contents

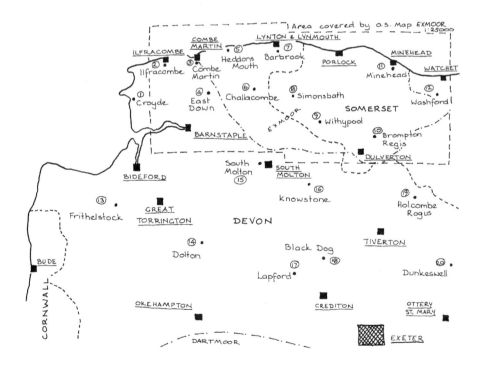

Area map showing the locations of the walks.

# Introduction

Exmoor and North Devon, together, have some of the loveliest countryside in England. From the moorlands and cliff scenery of 'Doone Country' to the wooded valleys of the Taw and Torridge rivers, made famous in the novel *Tarka the Otter*, the landscape is a joy to behold. It is also a walkers' paradise. The numerous footpaths are generally well signposted, the bridleways and farm tracks are clear and well used and the narrow lanes are often empty of traffic. In addition, the farmers are friendly and helpful to responsible ramblers, and the local pubs are well appointed and welcoming to visitors.

The walks in this book offer a range of routes across different types of terrain, from clifftop to moor, from meadow to wood. Many of the ones described include shorter or longer options. These will allow readers to adapt walks to suit themselves, or to undertake more than one route from each starting point. There are also suggestions, in the text, for other walks in the area and for other places to be visited, each pub listed acting as a focal point for numerous possible excursions.

The Ordnance Survey Maps referred to in the book form part of the Landranger series, 1:50 000 scale. Those visiting Exmoor may also like to use the OS Outdoor Leisure Map (1:25 000) which gives even more detail. All the rights of way mentioned should be walkable. Readers who find any difficulty with a public footpath should telephone the local authority, which is responsible for maintaining rights of way.

Generally pubs still keep 'normal' opening times – 11 am or 11.30 am to 2.30 pm, 6.30 pm or 7 pm to 11 pm. Sunday afternoon opening is now becoming common. Eating times tend to be 12 noon to 1.30 pm and 7 pm to 10 pm. Variations in these times are mentioned in the text. Most pubs have their own car parks and landlords allow customers to leave vehicles there while going for a short walk. However, it would be polite to ask those landlords first before doing so. All the establishments in this book welcome families with children, many having special 'family rooms' and gardens with play equipment. Nowadays, the quality and variety of food on offer in

7

pubs is exceptional, and all the places listed have menus that should satisfy even the most discerning of tastes and diets. Real ales are now widely available. The food and drink items listed in the pub profiles are, of course, given only as examples. Regular dishes and daily specials may vary with the time of year and changes in kitchen staff. The beers and ciders, too, may alter with contractual arrangements with breweries and suppliers.

I should like to thank all those pub proprietors who supplied me with valuable information about their establishments. I am also indebted to Glenys Jones for drawing the maps, and to Gwen Cassell who helped with the final draft.

Charles Whynne-Hammond
Spring 1996

**Publisher's Note**

We hope that you obtain considerable enjoyment from this book; great care has been taken in its preparation. However, changes of landlord and actual closures are sadly not uncommon. Likewise, although at the time of publication all routes followed public rights of way or permitted paths, diversion orders can be made and permissions withdrawn.

We cannot of course be held responsible for such diversion orders and any inaccuracies in the text which result from these or any other changes to the routes nor any damage which might result from walkers trespassing on private property. We are anxious though that all details covering the walks and the pubs are kept up to date and would therefore welcome information from readers which would be relevant to future editions.

# ① Croyde
## The Manor House Inn

As an attractive village, with old cottages and narrow streets, Croyde becomes highly congested during the holiday season. Most visitors seem to come here for the many good beaches nearby, but the countryside and cliff scenery in the vicinity should not be missed.

The Manor House Inn should not be missed either. It is old (formerly a 16th-century coaching inn), comfortable, friendly and – best of all – is open all day. Morning coffee and afternoon tea are served, as well as the usual pub fare, and families are especially welcome. There is even a ghost here; the apparition of a monk has been seen on several occasions.

This is a large establishment with separate sitting areas. There is a main bar, divided into different sections, a family room and a restaurant. Everywhere there are beams and bare stonework, and the walls are hung with various pictures and prints. Outside is a pleasant terrace-cum-beer garden.

Several different real ales are served, including Tetley and Boddingtons Bitter, two draught ciders (Inch's and Taunton) and a full

range of wines. The food, both regular menu items and daily specials written up on blackboards, is excellent. Ranging from toasted sandwiches, jacket potatoes, pasties and burgers to main course grills and fish dishes, the choice should suit everyone. Sweets include jam rolypoly and hot chocolate fudge cake – both delicious. Vegetarians are well catered for, with such meals as vegetable moussaka and cashew nut slice, and children have their own selection.
Telephone: 01271 890241.

*How to get there:* Facing Bideford Bay, in the northern extremity of Devon, Croyde seems a little isolated from the rest of the county. It stands west of the A361 Ilfracombe to Barnstaple road and can best be reached along the B3231 through Braunton. The Manor House Inn will be found towards the eastern end of Croyde.

*Parking:* There is a large pub car park – which is fortunate since there are few other places in Croyde where vehicles may be left. The lanes are narrow and, especially in summer, very busy. There are, however, several large public car parks down by the coast, around Croyde Bay.

*Length of the walk:* 3½ miles (shorter and longer options). OS map Landranger 180 Barnstaple and Ilfracombe (inn GR 447393).

*The whole coastline can be explored from Croyde, from Woolacombe to the Taw Estuary, and the coast path out to Baggy Point offers an excellent walking excursion. The views all around are superb; north to Morte Point, south towards the Clovelly coast and out to sea to Lundy Island. This circular walk extends to the hamlet of Saunton and back, via Saunton Down. The route is very clear throughout, using well worn paths across farmland and gravel trackways. There are some gradients to negotiate, but nothing strenuous enough to spoil your enjoyment of the walk.*

## The Walk

Turn right outside the Manor House Inn and walk down the road towards the centre of the village. Shortly before the road junction, turn left along Watery Lane, crossing the stream as you go. At the end turn left again and continue up the lane past Chuggs Farm. Beyond the last cottages go straight on, uphill, along a gravel track that runs

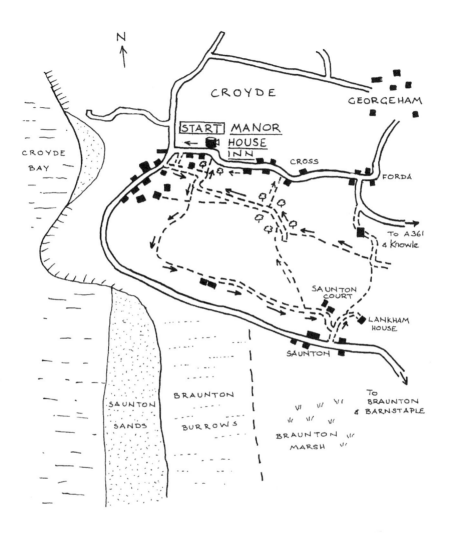

between hedgebanks. Soon this track turns right, then left. At the second bend you leave the track and go through the farm gate ahead. Cross the field diagonally (half-left), pass through a kissing-gate, and proceed to the bottom corner. Croyde Bay should be down to your right. Down at the next gate you meet a junction of paths. To the left is Lobbhill, to the right is Croyde, straight on is Saunton. Follow the way to Saunton and climb the stile.

The route is very easy to follow. The path is well trodden and

11

*Hillside view of Forda.*

regular stiles and signposts show the way. Essentially, you skirt the western slopes of the hill in front, first climbing, then descending as you curve round to Saunton. The hedge-bounded track becomes a path across grassland, as you continue over two stiles and contour along the hill slope. Up at the skyline you follow the direction indicated by the signpost. Cross two fields and then, bearing left, descend at an angle. On the ascent the views are back, north to Baggy Point. On the descent the views are ahead, down across the sweep of Braunton Burrows to the distant cliffs at Hartland Point. What a splendid panorama! The Burrows, which back onto Saunton Sands, form a vast dune-scape. These, in turn, are backed by Braunton Marsh, a fenland area of great importance as a nature reserve. Access is limited, since the area is also used by the Ministry of Defence.

At the bottom of the angled descent you continue past a derelict cottage, and follow the trackway signposted to Saunton Court, which will be reached after about ½ mile. Those wishing to shorten the circuit should turn left before Saunton Court and follow the path that leads north over the hilltop. Others should continue past Saunton Court, bearing right with the track and then turning left at the next junction, in the direction signposted to Lankham House (along a tarmac track).

Beyond Lankham House continue along the bridleway, this being a grassy track that climbs steadily uphill. It is bounded by hedgebanks and skirts the edge of a woodland. At the top, continue straight on at the junction of tracks, towards Forda but then, after just 30 yards, go through the gate on the left-hand side. Contour across the field to a stone step-stile and then head down across the following field, aiming to the left of Croyde Bay which is directly ahead. A further stile takes you onto a hedged pathway. Follow this downhill, bearing right at the clearer track that you meet, and in due course pass a barn.

Those wishing to lengthen their walk should turn right at the signpost pointing to Cross and then, down at the road, turn left. Others should continue. Soon the track turns right then left – a point to be recognised, since it was seen on the outward journey. But do not retrace your steps. At the second bend continue along a narrow earthy path. This curves left and descends steeply beneath the trees. At the bottom is the road. The Manor House Inn is just a few yards away.

## Places of interest nearby

In Croyde itself there are several places to visit, including the *Chapel Farm Gallery and Craft Centre*, the *Gem Rock and Shell Museum* and, down by the sea, *Cascades* adventure pool. At Woolacombe (3 miles north) is the *Once Upon a Time* theme park for children. Near Barnstaple (6 miles south-east) is the *Butterfly House* at *Ashford Gardens*.

# ② Ilfracombe
## The Royal Britannia Hotel

Ilfracombe is a large and popular holiday resort with all the usual tourist attractions. However, it is much prettier than many others in England. It nestles amongst hills and high sea cliffs and its busy little harbour is dominated by a medieval chapel that stands on top of Lantern Hill. Many of the buildings are old and interesting, dating from Tudor times.

The Royal Britannia Hotel, overlooking the quay, itself occupies a grand 'listed' building of 18th-century proportions. Lord Nelson is reputed to have stayed here. The interior is traditional in style and decorated with many pictures of a nautical theme. It is a large building, so there is plenty of room to spread out. There are three main bars together with other sitting areas. On the harbour side is a terrace which is most popular in summer months.

But the Royal Britannia should be visited for more reasons than just its historic associations. It is open all day, has a friendly, comfortable atmosphere and serves a wonderful range of refreshments.

Morning coffee and afternoon tea are served, John Smith's and Courage Best ales are offered, draught cider and various wines are also available. The menus are wide-ranging in both cost and content, with both regular items and numerous daily specials listed to tempt every palate. From sandwiches, salads and items with chips, the range becomes more imaginative with pies, grills, pasta dishes and roasts. The fish is especially inviting, much of it being locally caught, such as cod, plaice, haddock, Dover sole, prawns, mussels and cockles. Vegetarians should have no problem choosing from the list of pasta and vegetable bakes. Children have their own menu too.

Telephone: 01271 862939.

*How to get there:* Ilfracombe is not hard to find; it lies on the coast just a few miles from the western edge of the Exmoor National Park, and is easily reached from Barnstaple (10 miles south). The Royal Britannia faces Broad Street on one side and the harbour on the other.

*Parking:* Being a town centre establishment there is no pub car park. However, there are numerous pay and display public car parks throughout Ilfracombe. Free parking, in side streets, would be easier out of season.

*Length of the walk:* 3 miles (shorter and longer options). OS map Landranger 180 Barnstaple and Ilfracombe (inn GR 523478).

*The coastline either side of Ilfracombe is spectacular and many fine walks can be enjoyed along the coast path. To the west is Torrs Park, where there is a network of clifftop paths. The walk beyond here, to Lee Bay (2 miles away), is also a popular excursion. This walk begins along the coast path east of Ilfracombe, across a headland known as the Hillsborough Leisure Area. From there it drops down to Hele Bay and then returns more inland using, for the most part, grassy trackways. Route finding is not difficult but some steep gradients are involved. The views to be enjoyed should amply reward the exertion.*

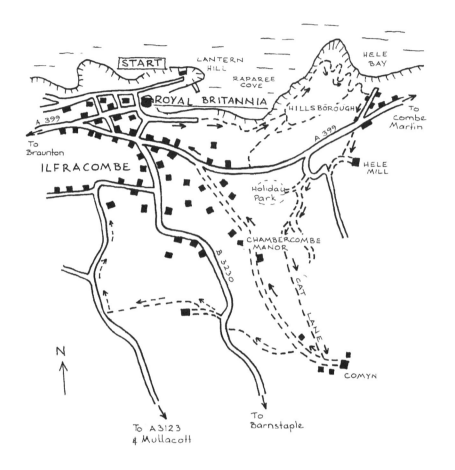

## The Walk

The way to Hele Bay is not difficult to find, for it is a well worn and well signposted route. If in doubt, whenever a choice of paths is offered, keep to the seaward side as you skirt the headland. Those wishing to walk simply to Hele Bay and back (a total distance of 2 miles) could use the clifftop path on the outward journey and the direct path back, around the landward side of the hill. To reach Hillsborough headland from the Royal Britannia, walk along by the harbour, up through the long stay car park and then left down via the pitch-and-putt hut to Raparee Cove. From there, keeping to the clifftop, climb up along the edge of the pitch-and-putt course and then, through a gate and a belt of trees, onward along a clear path across the grassland. Soon you will meet a wider track. Follow this to the left.

There are fine views to be had from Hillsborough, along the coast in both directions. As you descend, on the eastern side you will find a viewpoint which contains an information board. This gives a pictorial guide to the seabirds flying around – a useful aid. From there the path zigzags down all the way to Hele Bay, where you will find a public convenience and ice-cream shop.

From Hele walk up Beach Road, unless of course you intend to return directly to Ilfracombe. At the main road go straight over, along the footpath that begins next to the bus stop. This leads beside a stream and emerges at Hele Mill. Those with time to spare should certainly look inside, for it is a restored watermill where wholemeal flour is made and sold. From here continue up the track to the road, turn right, then left and then – where the road bends again – straight on towards Hele Valley Holiday Park. Do not, however, walk past the caravans. Just before the campsite shop turn left, up a narrow lane marked as a dead-end and called Cat Lane. This is a Private Road, but is a right of way for walkers.

The tarmac surface soon becomes tarmac and grass as it climbs steadily. It swings right and then, a little further on, sharply left. At this point, continue straight on, along a dark, earthy trackway that runs between deep hedgebanks. This offers a pleasant walk, with glimpses of the valley down to the right through the trees. At the far end you reach a farmstead (called Comyn). After the first gate turn sharp right and then continue round through another gate to follow a tarmac lane that runs beneath the trees. This track will eventually take you back to the eastern end of Ilfracombe.

Those wishing to lengthen their circular walk by ½ mile should be prepared for some steep ascents through dense undergrowth. Just before the house on the right take the path that climbs steeply up through the woodland on the left. Towards the top bear right to reach the main road. Turn right, downhill, but then turn left opposite the Recycling Centre. Continue round behind the farm, through some paddocks and on beside some playing fields. Beyond the next field you reach the road. Turn right and, soon after, right again to return to Ilfracombe town centre.

*Ilfracombe harbour.*

## Places of interest nearby

Ilfracombe has all the usual attractions of a holiday centre. The *Museum and Brass Rubbing Centre* is especially interesting. From the harbour, sea fishing trips operate, together with pleasure cruises and a seasonal ferry to Lundy Island. At Mullacott (2 miles south) is the *Miniature Ponies and Shire Horse Centre*.

# Combe Martin
## The Dolphin Inn

**3**

If you come to the Exmoor coast you should visit Combe Martin for it is a pleasant little town combining the varied amusements of a holiday resort with the picturesque bustle of a Devon fishing harbour. And if you come to Combe Martin you should visit the Dolphin Inn, for it is the most friendly and well appointed of pubs.

The building is much older inside than it looks from the outside. There is a low, beamed ceiling, a large open fireplace and much traditional woodwork. It is decorated with dried flowers and photos of old Combe Martin. Beyond the main bar is another room which houses the pool table and leads through to the patio. To the right is a separate lounge. The owners have deeds to the property that go back to 1690, and it is said that, in 1704, the pub was sold for the grand sum of half-a-crown!

A wide variety of drinks is offered, including many real ales, for example, John Smith's Bitter and Courage Directors, numerous stouts, draught ciders like Scrumpy Jack and a range of wines. But it is the variety – and quality – of the food served that makes the Dolphin

Inn stand out. Apart from regular items, like sandwiches, ploughman's lunches, burgers, salads, pies and so on, there are daily specials, these being written up on blackboards both inside and on the pavement. And what a choice! Fish dishes include lobster, salmon, parrot fish and monkfish; meat courses feature Exmoor venison, steaks, chicken, pork and – sometimes – even Canadian bison. The sweets are wonderfully traditional, like apple pie and ice cream. Vegetarians have many salads and pasta dishes to choose from and children have their own menu.

Normal pub opening times are kept.

Telephone: 01271 883424.

*How to get there:* Combe Martin stands on the coast just 4 miles east of Ilfracombe, at the western edge of the Exmoor National Park. Barnstaple is 10 miles away to the south. The Dolphin Inn will be found, overlooking the harbour, on the main A399.

*Parking:* Because of its central position, and the nature of Combe Martin's cluster of buildings, the Dolphin Inn has just a very small car park. Elsewhere in town – notably at the far (eastern) side of the harbour – pay meter parking is provided. There is also a large free car park near the church, halfway up the High Street going inland.

*Length of the walk:* 3 miles (longer option). OS map Landranger 18 Barnstaple and Ilfracombe (inn GR 577473).

*The coastal scenery on either side of Combe Martin is spectacular and good walks can be had in both directions, along the South West Coast Path. To the east this footpath climbs steeply up to Great Hangman, from where panoramic views may be enjoyed by those fit enough to make the ascent. The walk described here is suitable for those wishing to take a less strenuous excursion. The coast path is followed west and then country lanes are used to explore the delightful village of Berrynarbor. Some gradients are encountered but nothing that should be too arduous.*

## The Walk

The coast path out of Combe Martin is well signposted so route finding should not be a problem. Simply take your time and enjoy the views along the coast, especially those back across Combe Martin

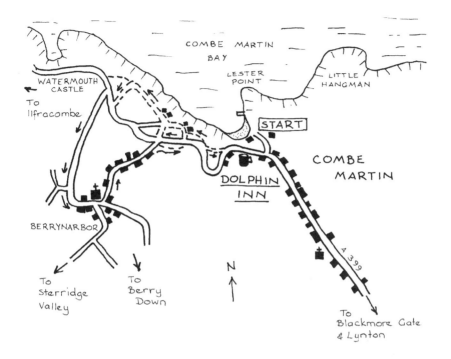

Bay. Walk uphill from the Dolphin, along the main road as it bends left, and then turn right down Newberry Road. This passes round the back of some cottages and their gardens, and then swings right to climb steeply. At the top you rejoin the main road and continue along this out of town. Soon you reach a couple of pedestrian gates that lead you through to a footpath. This climbs along the edge of a field, separated from the road by a hedgerow. At the far end a flight of steps takes you up to a lane. Once the coast path went right here, along the lane, but nowadays it rejoins the main road, which you must follow for another few hundred yards. You are still climbing but at least a grass verge keeps you away from the traffic.

Opposite the road that goes left to Berrynarbor turn right down a tarmac lane. This leads to a point where many hotel drives converge. Continue half-left along Old Coast Road. This is metalled at first but becomes a gravel track soon after passing some cottages. Old Coast Road offers an easy walk through woodlands and around the headland. Below, through the trees, is the sea. You keep to this trackway all the way round until you meet, once again, the main road. Opposite the caravan site, which soon appears to your left, there is a coast path sign pointing right. Ignore this, unless, of course, you wish to keep to the cliff edge and visit Watermouth Castle a mile away.

Having left the route of the South West Coast Path you now head for Berrynarbor. Take the lane almost opposite when you reach the main road. This runs downhill below the trees and then, at the bottom of the combe, swings left to climb steeply to the main part of the village. Berrynarbor is justly popular amongst tourists. Old cottages straggle down the wooded hill slope below the 15th-century church and all the gardens are prettily maintained. There is a free car park, and public conveniences, and those seeking refreshment can visit either Ye Olde Globe pub or Miss Muffet's Tearoom. Those wishing to extend their circular walk should amble around the village lanes.

The return to Combe Martin begins up Barton Hill, north from the church. This becomes Barton Lane and you follow it all the way to the main road. You do not, however, turn down the main road. Immediately before the junction, follow the direction indicated by the footpath signpost. This means climbing a stile and following the edge of a field. Three more stiles, another field and a length of woodland track will bring you back to the main road. Cross over and retrace the coast path route you followed at the start of the walk. The Dolphin awaits at the bottom of the hill.

## Places of interest nearby

All manner of attractions can be found in Combe Martin itself, including a *Motorcycle Museum* and – at the top end – the *Wildlife and Dinosaur Park*. Along the coast westwards is *Watermouth Castle*, a mock-Gothic building now converted to a theme park for children. Here there are model demonstrations, 'gnomeland' and 'dungeon' experiences, and all kinds of family facilities.

# **East Down**
## 4 The Pyne Arms

The small attractive village of East Down, clinging to a steep valley slope, stands close to the National Trust property of Arlington Court. And, not surprisingly, many of the visitors to that estate come to the Pyne Arms for rest and refreshment. They are never disappointed, for this pub offers exceptional service, in comfort, hospitality and food. Sadly, the place keeps only to normal pub opening times.

Belonging to the Exmoor Inns group, the Pyne Arms occupies a building that dates back, at least, to Stuart times. It is much bigger inside than it looks from outside. There are low beamed ceilings, walls hung with hunting prints, old posters and pictures of rural scenes, and areas of bare stone. The one bar room is so arranged that separate areas have been created, one housing the pool table, another being more of a dining room. Outside there is a terraced beer garden, where children sit when the no smoking area inside is full, or when the weather is especially fine.

The real ales served include John Smith's Bitter and Courage Directors, the draught cider is Dry Blackthorn, and various wines are

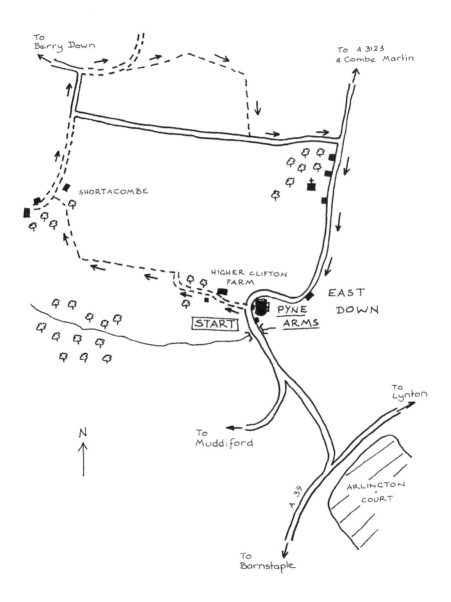

To Berry Down

To A 3123 & Combe Martin

SHORTACOMBE

HIGHER CLIFTON FARM

EAST DOWN

PYNE ARMS

START

N

To Lynton

To Muddiford

A 39

ARLINGTON COURT

To Barnstaple

listed. But you can hardly come to the Pyne Arms without sampling the food! It is superb in both variety and quality. A large regular menu is supplemented by daily specials written up on a number of blackboards, and great pride is taken with the local nature of the produce. There are snacks and light meals (sandwiches, jacket potatoes and salads), main dishes (grills, pies, casseroles and roasts), and tempting desserts (flans, ice-creams and cakes). In season, mussels are available, and the salmon dishes are especially good. Vegetarians also have an excellent choice, from pasta bakes to mushroom stroganoff.

Telephone: 01271 850207.

*How to get there:* East Down stands just off the A39, between Blackmore Gate and Barnstaple. It is very close to the western boundary of the Exmoor National Park and Combe Martin is only 4 miles away to the north. The Pyne Arms will be found at the southern end of the village, downhill from the church and manor house.

*Parking:* There is a large pub car park on the opposite side of the road. Parking space elsewhere in the village is very limited, the lanes being narrow, steep and winding.

*Length of the walk:* 2½ miles. OS map Landranger 180 Barnstaple and Ilfracombe (inn GR 600414).

*The Arlington Court estate, just a mile away, has landscaped parkland in which many walks are possible. There is also a nature trail by the lake. The adjoining woodlands, down the upper Yeo valley, are also owned by the National Trust and these too offer ample walking possibilities. This short circular walk crosses the more open area west of East Down, where farmland covers the rolling hills. Rights of way are used across this agricultural landscape, although the paths themselves are not always very clear. There are stiles to negotiate, some requiring a little agility. However, the ground underfoot is generally dry throughout. The views are intimate and pleasant.*

### The Walk

Walk downhill from the Pyne Arms and, after just a few yards, turn right along an old concrete track. A footpath signpost points the way and another sign reads Higher Clifton Farm. Continue to the farm

25

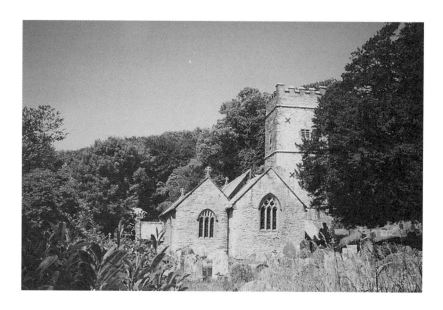

*East Down church.*

itself where, on the far side of the farmyard, you will see a metal gate. This leads through to another trackway. This one is gravel surfaced and tractor-rutted. It runs between hedgebanks, under some trees and, in due course, swings right along a field edge. It offers a very pleasant start to the walk, and you should follow it with relaxed pleasure. In summer months the wild flowers are a joy.

At the top end this track ends at a number of farm gates, close to a large corrugated iron barn. At this point turn left through one of the gates and follow the field edge along, keeping the hedgerow on your left. In the next corner are two more gates. Go through the one on the left and follow the top edge of the next field, keeping the hedgerow this time to your right. The view down to the left, across the wooded combe, is attractive. The valley is a tributary of the river Yeo. In the far corner some rough stone steps will take you over a stile, situated on top of the hedgebank. On the far side a vertical wooden step-stile takes you over a tall wire fence. From this point the public right of way actually cuts diagonally half-right across the field, but you may be directed around by the hedge, straight on then right. In either case you reach the hamlet of Shortacombe. Follow the earthy track running beneath the trees and then, at the first house, swing sharp right. The firm drive will lead you back and round, past another house, and up to the road. When you reach the road continue straight on, until you come to the next bend. Here the road turns left to Berry Down and a tarmac track goes right to Beccot. Follow the latter direction. A footpath signpost confirms that this is a right of way.

Where the track bears left, however, you leave the tarmac and go through the gate in front. Cross the field diagonally half-left, to a gate in the far corner. In the following field go diagonally half-right. This is not a rectangular field. Do *not* aim for the corner with a small tree, head for the farther one to its left. There you will find a gate followed, almost immediately, by a stile. Through the third and last field head down to the bottom left-hand corner. There some stone steps take you onto the top of the hedgebank. More stone steps lead you down the far side to the road. Be careful here. In summer the vegetation can be dense. On the road turn left to return to East Down. Those with spare time should look around the predominantly 15th-century church. They will find it behind the trees next to the Manor House. It contains some monuments to the Pine, or Pyne, family, which once owned the estate here. It is through this connection, of course, that we now have 'The Pyne Arms'.

## Places of interest nearby
Apart from *Arlington Court*, with its carriage collection and Victorian gardens, nature lovers should visit *Wistlandpound Reservoir*, 3 miles to the east. It is an excellent spot for both fishing and bird-watching. Just 3 miles north-west of East Down, at Bodstone Barton, is *Farm World and Playland*, a farming theme park especially designed for children.

# ⑤ Heddon's Mouth
## The Hunters Inn

There is no village here, but the Heddon Valley is one of the most popular tourist destinations along the Exmoor coast. There is a large car park, a National Trust shop and public conveniences. Most of the valley is owned by the National Trust and there are numerous woodland paths to explore, some of these extending down to the coast where there is a small beach. And all around the scenery is breathtaking, with deep wooded combes cutting like Swiss gorges through the bare moorland heights that rise 800 feet above sea level.

The Hunters Inn serves visitors well. It is open all day, serving coffees in the morning, pub fare at lunchtimes and teas in the afternoons. In the evenings it acts as a good restaurant. This large Edwardian building replaces an old, thatched farmhouse that was, sadly, burned down at the end of the 19th century. Inside, there are comfortable cushioned chairs and tables with tablecloths, walls decorated with old photographs and hunting theme ornaments, and a chimney-piece containing a wood-burner. Children are welcome and everyone is treated with friendliness.

Many real ales are offered, like Exmoor Ale and St Austell HSD, and locally-made cider is available on tap. Various wines are also served. All the food is wholesome and home-made, and very good value. Regular items, like sandwiches, ploughman's lunches, salads, steaks and fish dishes are supplemented by daily specials written up on the blackboard. Despite the name and theme of the place, vegetarian food is also provided, for example, beanburgers and vegetable pancake rolls.

Telephone: 01598 763230.

*How to get there:* The Heddon Valley runs from Parracombe to the sea, about halfway between Combe Martin and Lynton/Lynmouth. Due to the rugged nature of the landscape it is not crossed by any main roads, the closest being the A39 at Parracombe. It can also be reached from the A399 Combe Martin road.

*Parking:* The Hunters Inn car park is generally used by those enjoying the hotel facilities. But there is plenty of car space else-where, either along the roadside in front, or in the public car park 100 yards up on the right.

*Length of the walk:* 2½ miles. OS map Landranger 180 Barnstaple and Ilfracombe (inn GR 655482).

*This walk, although fairly short, can be strenuous since it involves some steep gradients and a short section along the edge of a clifftop. The route is perfectly safe but requires energy and a head for heights. The coast path is followed westwards and the return route incor-porates the pretty hamlet of Trentishoe. For those wanting a less demanding walk there is plenty of choice, as riverside paths meander through the woods both up and down the valley. Many people, of all ages, walk down to the beach and back, a total distance of about 2 miles.*

## The Walk

Follow the track that runs along the eastern side of the Hunters Inn, to the right as you look at the building from the front. The signpost points the way to Martinhoe, Woody Bay and – the direction you want initially – Heddon's Mouth. A little further along take the left fork, which descends through the woods.

29

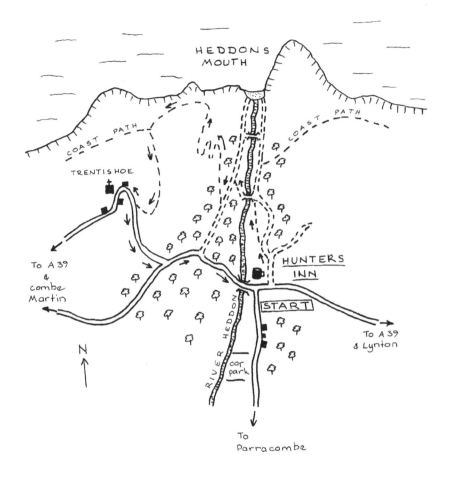

Being owned by the National Trust, these woods have numerous paths, on both sides of the river. Many visitors walk down to the coast along one bank and return along the other. The path downstream, close to the watercourse itself, is especially pretty. In due course you reach a large wooden footbridge. Cross the river and continue along the other bank, on a path that runs through a gate and joins another wider track. This other track follows the valley side along all the way to the beach. Those heading that way should continue seawards. Those intent on the more strenuous circuit should turn left and follow this track back up the valley. After a short while you reach a gate. Continue through this and keep to the track for another 300 or

400 yards. You will soon see a signpost on your right pointing back, uphill. This is the coast path to Combe Martin and is the route you want.

The coast path is well worn and very clear, but it is also steep. At first it climbs through the woods, then it winds up in zigzags across the bracken. Here and there, at the steepest points, rough wooden steps help your ascent. Wonderful views soon open out, to the right across the combe and down to the jagged cliffs above the beach. After climbing up beside a side gully the path veers seawards to contour around the headland. At the far end you turn the corner and look out to the open sea, Heddon's Mouth itself now being far below to the right-hand side. Continue along the coast, following a stony, clifftop path. Take care along this stretch, for the waves are a long way below. Soon the view westwards appears, and you can see the distant Widmouth Head, beyond Combe Martin. Round the next corner a further ascent brings you up to a boundary fence, marking the edge of the farmland beyond. From this point the coast path continues to the right but you turn left, following the signpost arm pointing the way to Trentishoe church.

The route to Trentishoe is now easy. Follow this path all the way, along the top of the steep valley side that dips down to the Heddon river. The stone wall and fence marking the edge of the fields should be on your right. Along this stretch you can see Hunters Inn, way down in the valley bottom. Indeed, all the views are splendid. In due course the grassy path dips down to meet a lane. Turn right, uphill, to visit Trentishoe before returning, downhill, to walk back to Hunters Inn (turning left at the bottom). Trentishoe is a delightful hamlet with a few farm cottages clustered below a small church; it should not be missed.

### Places of interest nearby

*Parracombe*, a village 3 miles upstream along the Heddon valley, is a lovely spot, with two attractive churches. The older of the two dates back to the 12th century. Nearby is a walk along a section of the disused Lynton and Barnstaple Railway, a Victorian narrow gauge line built for tourists. *Woody Bay* (2 miles east) has spectacular cliff scenery and is owned by the National Trust.

# Challacombe
**6** The Black Venus

Challacombe is an isolated village set amongst the rolling moorlands of Exmoor's loneliest region. The bleak ridge, known as The Chains, stands above it. But it is a busy little place, largely because visitors come to sample the culinary delights of the Black Venus. And well they might, for this pub's fame is well deserved.

It is a lovely old building with a warm, cosy atmosphere. There are low beamed ceilings, plain walls hung with pictures and, at one end, a great fireplace with stone mantel surround. The poolroom is separate, as too is the large dining room. Youngsters are welcome in the latter, part of which is a no smoking area.

Owned by Exmoor Inns, which also runs the pubs at East Down and Blackmoor Gate (both further west), the Black Venus boasts a large and exceptionally varied menu. Apart from a regular selection, offering all manner of sandwiches, salads, steaks, fish dishes and pasta courses, daily specials are listed on blackboards. These include local delicacies like trout and lamb, various stir-fry meals and home-made pies. One blackboard is entirely devoted to vegetarian snacks listing, among others, cheese and vegetable bakes and meatless burgers. Another blackboard lists desserts which supplement the cake choice in the display cabinet.

Normal pub opening times are kept. The real ales served include John Smith's Bitter, Webster's Yorkshire Bitter and Ushers Triple Crown, and the draught ciders available are Dry Blackthorn and Cidermaster. As one would expect of such an establishment the wine list is comprehensive.

Telephone: 01598 763251.

*How to get there:* Challacombe stands on the B3358, 5 miles west of Simonsbath. Lynton and the coast lie 6 miles north, across the open moor. By road the village is most easily reached from the A399 Combe Martin to South Molton road, turning east near Blackmoor Gate. The Black Venus stands at the northern end of the village.

*Parking:* There is a large pub car park, across the road. There is also a long layby nearby where cars may be left.

*Length of the walk:* 2½ miles. OS map Landranger 180 Barnstaple and Ilfracombe (inn GR 694411).

*Challacombe provides an excellent centre for many walks. There are large areas of open moorland to the north-east and two long distance footpaths can be reached just a few miles east, namely the Tarka Trail and the Two Moors Way. The views from some of the nearby summits are spectacular; west to the north Devon coast, south to Dartmoor. This short walk offers a more gentle option – a stroll across farmland and around the upper tributaries of the river Bray. The route follows a footpath to Challacombe church, returning along a bridleway. The way is clearly marked throughout, with regular signposts and direction indicators. Some stiles need to be climbed but no real obstacles exist. The gradients are also fairly gentle.*

## The Walk

Strangely, Challacombe church is over a mile away from Challacombe village. It stands at the hamlet of Barton Town. To reach it, walk down the road opposite the Black Venus, across the ford (using the footbridge nearby), and on past the Methodist chapel. Ignoring the first footpath signpost you see on the right, follow the way marked by the

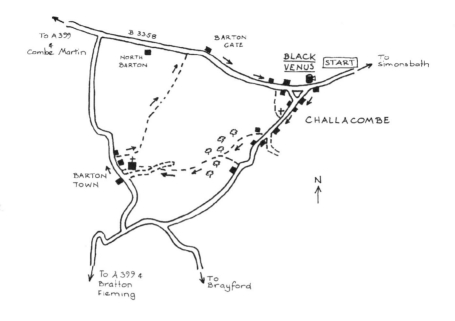

second, located next to the gate for Home Place Farm Holiday Cottages and arrowed 'Footpath to Challacombe Church'. Through a further gate a very clear grassy path continues across the meadows and behind a field which, in summer, is used by caravans. Over a small side stream, using stepping-stones, continue alongside a woodland keeping the river down to your left. In due course you reach another footpath signpost. As directed, continue up through the wood. This is a steady ascent but is not very arduous. At the top is a gate and another signpost. Continue straight on across the pasture fields.

There are, in fact, three fields to cross before you reach a farm track. Across these you go up, down and then up again, by which time you should be able to see the church directly ahead, its tower set amongst a group of trees. Go straight over the farm track and cross two more small fields. Most of Challacombe church was rebuilt in 1850 but the tower is original Gothic, providing a pleasant backdrop to the overgrown graveyard. Indeed, this is an attractive spot generally with a few cottages and farms clinging to a green hillside. Barton Town – as this tiny hamlet is called – was probably much more important once than it is today, acting as a focal point for a scatter of homesteads. 'Barton' comes from the Saxon words for 'barley farm'.

The journey back to Challacombe follows a bridleway that links Barton Town with North Barton and Barton Gate, along a route that evidently has some historic significance. It is thought this could be the line of a former drove road. It probably formed part of a trackway linking Bratton Fleming in the south with Lynton and Lynmouth in the north. From the church walk down to the road, turn right (uphill) and then, after just 50 yards, right again. The bridleway sign will be seen pointing along a track that runs between the back wall of the churchyard and, on the left, some large modern barns. The intervening gates have blue-painted squares indicating the way. Beyond these, a wide hedgebanked trackway leads onwards. At the top continue through the next gate and then along the edge of a field, keeping the hedgebank to your left. By now the views have opened out ahead. After the next gate aim diagonally half-right, the path being clearly visible between grassy banks. The gate in the far corner of the following field brings you to the road. Turn right, pass a house called Barton Gate and continue back to Challacombe.

## Places of interest nearby

In Challacombe village itself, up the road from the Black Venus, is the *Poppins Bird Sanctuary* where visitors can see the work involved in the care of such birds as swans, owls and kestrels. *Arlington Court* (5 miles west) is a National Trust property with a house, gardens and a carriage collection. The *Exmoor Steam Railway* (3 miles south-west) is a must for locomotive enthusiasts, and the *Exmoor Animal and Bird Gardens* (3 miles west) is a must for ornithologists.

# Barbrook
### ⑦ The Beggars Roost Inn

There is quite a holiday complex here. The Channel View Caravan Park, together with its general store, shares a road front with the Manor Hotel which, itself, incorporates the Gallery Restaurant and the Beggars Roost Inn. Thus, even out of pub opening times, refreshments are always available – ice-cream, morning coffee or afternoon tea.

The hotel end of the building, of course, was once the manor house, dating back to the 17th century. The pub end was once a barn. Both have been converted traditionally, and to a high standard of comfort. The latter consists of a long, dark bar room with bare brick walls and wood panelling, these decorated with plates, pictures and brassware. There is also a large open fireplace – very cosy in winter.

The real ales served include Cotleigh Tawny Bitter and Tetley Bitter, the draught cider is Addlestones, and there is a full wine list. A full bar menu is supplemented by daily blackboard specials, and there should be something for everyone, even vegetarians. Snacks include jacket potatoes, with various fillings, burgers and pasties; main courses feature chicken Kiev, steak and kidney pie, cod and plaice, and lasagne verdi. Desserts include apple pie, ice cream and orange sorbet. Children have their own menu. The Sunday roasts prove very popular and there is also a carvery.

The Beggars Roost Inn, as opposed to the hotel, keeps normal pub opening times, but these may vary a little in the holiday season. All in all, a most pleasant place to stop.

Telephone: 01598 752404.

*How to get there:* Barbrook stands on the edge of Lynton, at the point where the B3234 joins the A39. The West Lyn river flows through the hamlet and steep wooded slopes rise up on either side. The Beggars Roost Inn will be found on the hilltop east of Barbrook, about a mile away on the A39 in the Porlock direction.

*Parking:* There is a large car park in front of the pub. Vehicles should not be left on the busy A39, but a few roadside spaces may be found along the lane to West Lyn Farm, where the walk begins.

*Length of the walk:* 2 miles (3½ miles longer option). OS map Landranger 180 Barnstaple and Ilfracombe (inn GR 724482).

*The valleys of the East and West Lyn rivers are spectacularly beautiful and many excellent walks can be undertaken from Barbrook. The nearby cliff scenery should also be explored, using the coast path from Lynton and Lynmouth. From Barbrook village itself, a good circular walk heads up the West Lyn valley and returns via Sparhanger and Furzehill. From Manor Hotel this circular walk goes seawards and offers wonderful views down to Lynmouth, and along the deep wooded cleaves towards Watersmeet. It is a very easy walk with no steep gradients, no stiles and no problems with route finding. Those wishing to extend their walk, and their enjoyment, can add another 1½ miles to the circuit.*

## The Walk

Walk up the lane that runs past the eastern end of Manor Hotel to West Lyn Farm. There, where the lane bends sharp right, a footpath signpost will be seen, close to the wall of a barn. The direction you want is straight on, to Summer House Hill. Past the farm buildings,

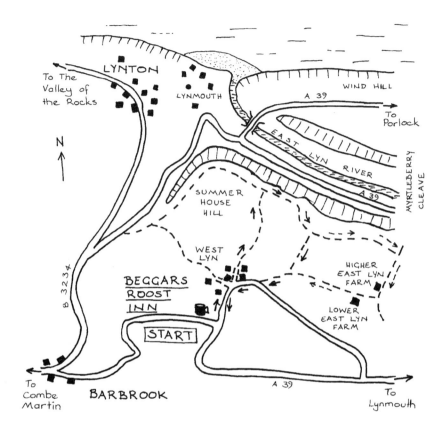

seawards, the track runs through a gate and on between the hedge-rows to another gate. Thereafter, follow the edge of a field, keeping the hedgerow to the left. At the bottom corner a small gate takes you through to the open moorland. The footpath you now join feels and looks like a high coastal path. But it is not a cliff that lies below, it is the deeply cut East Lyn valley. The coast actually lies ahead, beyond the next hill spur.

The views now become even more spectacular than before. Down to the left, far below, is Lynmouth harbour. To the right is Wind Hill and, beyond, the headland mass that runs out to Foreland Point. Turn right and follow the grassy path in the direction of Watersmeet, as indicated by the footpath signpost. Keep to the higher path at each of the next occasions when other paths lead down to the left. These go down to Lynmouth. The path you want accompanies the wall that divides the open moorland pasture from the farmland fields. Soon the views to the left extend all the way down Lyn Cleave and Myrtleberry Cleave – deep clefts cut by the East Lyn river. Dense woodland covers each side and the cars that move along the A39, at the bottom, look surprisingly small. In fact, the drop is some 800 feet. Most of the East Lyn valley along this stretch – to Watersmeet and beyond – is owned by the National Trust and there are many walks to be enjoyed through the woods and along by the river bank. This area deserves an extended stay.

The path you are following happens to be part of both the Two Moors Way (which runs right across Devon), and the Tarka Trail. The latter is a long distance path through the Taw and Torridge valleys, a landscape made famous by Henry Williamson in his book *Tarka the Otter*. In less than ½ mile, and after a slight ascent, you will see a grassy track leading off to the right. It runs between hedgebanks to a gate and then continues. Those keeping to the circuit as planned should follow this track. It goes all the way back to the lane near West Lyn Farm, turning sharp right on its way. Those wishing to extend their walk should continue along the top of the valley for another ½ mile. Another track can then be followed through Higher East Lyn Farm and Lower East Lyn Farm. This track rejoins the other one and leads down to the lane. At the lane turn right, to return to the Beggars Roost Inn.

## Places of interest nearby

The twin towns of Lynton and Lynmouth should not be missed. They are linked by a cliff railway and have many old and interesting buildings. Lynton contains the *Lyn and Exmoor Museum*, Lynmouth has the *Exmoor Brass Rubbing and Hobbycraft Centre*. Along the coast west of these towns is the *Valley of the Rocks*, a local beauty spot.

# ⑧ Simonsbath
## The Exmoor Forest Hotel

What a beautiful spot this hotel occupies, nestling in a wooded valley at the heart of the Exmoor National Park. Not surprisingly, many people find their way here. The Exmoor Forest has been a hotel for more than a century but the building it occupies – once two cottages built for estate workers – probably dates back to the 17th century. Inside, all is traditional with cushioned settles, wooden tables and walls adorned with stag heads, hunting pictures and old chinaware. There are wood-burners, used in winter months, so the atmosphere is always cosy and welcoming.

This freehouse dispenses real ales, including Exmoor Ale and Cotleigh Tawny, draught Gaymers Olde English cider and a range of wines. But it is the food served that makes this place so popular. Regular menu items are supplemented by daily specials, written on the blackboards above the bar counter. Bar snacks range from soups, sandwiches and jacket potatoes to salads and meals with chips; main courses include various meat pies, fish dishes and casseroles. The salmon and lamb meals are especially good. Vegetarians can choose from vegetable chilli, lasagne and various bakes, and children have their own little menu selection.

There is one bar but many rooms lead off at different levels, up and down short flights of steps. Outside there is a pleasant sitting area. Normal pub opening times are kept, but the hotel operation stays open in summertime to serve afternoon cream teas. Those wishing to stay at the Exmoor Forest Hotel could find no better centre from which to explore the surrounding countryside.

Telephone: 01643 83341.

*How to get there:* Simonsbath will be found at the junction of many roads: the B3223 from Wheddon Cross and Exford, the B3358 from Blackmoor Gate, the moorland 'Kinsford Gate' road that comes up from Brayford. It is most easily reached from the Lynton direction, leaving the A39 coast road near Watersmeet. The Exmoor Forest Hotel will be found at the eastern end of Simonsbath.

*Parking:* The hotel has a car park. There is also a large public car park, with public conveniences, a little to the east of the hotel, off the road to Exford.

*Simonsbath church.*

*Length of the walk:* 3½ miles. OS map Landranger 180 Barnstaple and Ilfracombe (inn GR 774394).

*Simonsbath stands along the upper reaches of the river Barle and, in consequence, has become a popular centre for those walkers exploring the Barle valley landscape. There is an excellent walk, 8 miles long, that follows the footpath downstream along the river bank to Cow Castle (an Iron Age fort), and then returns by way of a track that now forms part of the Two Moors Way. The walk suggested here, however, is rather shorter. It explores the open landscape north of Simonsbath. The route follows one tributary valley up to Prayway Head (from where there are wide views) and another tributary valley back. The footpaths used are not official public rights of way but are 'permitted paths', or ways which landowners allow the public to use. They are, nevertheless, clearly marked and easy to follow.*

## The Walk

The walk begins from the public car park which stands at the eastern end of Simonsbath, signposted from the Exford road. This car park is laid out in two levels. From the upper level a footpath is signposted to Prayway Head. This climbs fairly steeply through the trees and is the route to follow. The path is very clear as it climbs, and then levels off, to run along the top edge of the woodland. In due course it dips down to the left and crosses a small side stream, stepping-stones allowing walkers to cross. A gate beyond displays a yellow-painted arrow pointing the way ahead. Leaving the trees behind climb at an angle across the sloping pasture.

The route along this stretch is well marked by yellow-topped posts. All the while the attractive valley known as Ashcombe Bottom runs parallel and below you to the left. In the top corner a gate leads you through to a little side combe or damp hollow. Contour round this to continue your original direction – a signpost points the way. Now walk up the grassy hill to the skyline, keeping a tree-topped hedge-bank parallel over to your left. Aim for the top corner where another gate awaits. This takes you onto the open moor. This moorland, here being rough pasture rather than heather, has 'access land' status. Although privately owned, it is open to walkers who can roam (within reason) at will. Immediately after the gate turn left and follow the boundary wall west all the way to the road. But hurry not, as the views are getting better all the time. At the road turn right (northwards) in

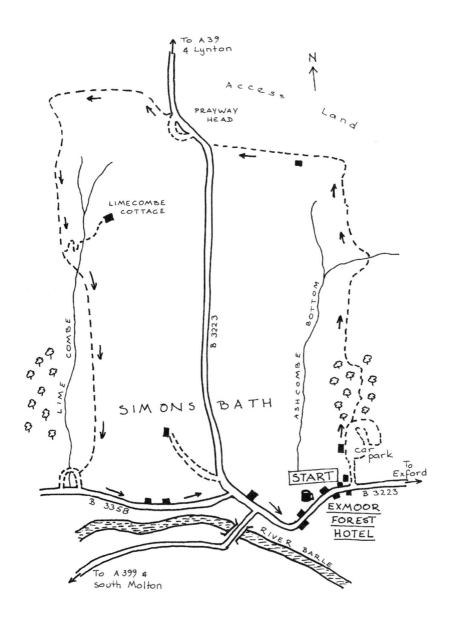

TO A39
4 Lynton

N

Access Land

PRAYWAY HEAD

LIMECOMBE COTTAGE

B 3223

ASHCOMBE BOTTOM

LIME COMBE

SIMONSBATH

car park

START

To Exford

B 3223

EXMOOR FOREST HOTEL

B 3358

RIVER BARLE

To A399 &
South Molton

43

order to reach a small car parking area. It is only about 200 yards away and consists of a curved layby on the left-hand side. Next to this layby is a footpath signpost, pointing the way to Dure Down. Follow this, the route being along the edge of a large field with the hedge-bank on your right. In the top corner go through the gate and turn immediately left. Keep the hedge now to your left.

The return to Simonsbath is well marked by signposts and yellow-topped posts. Avoiding the sheep pens in the bottom corner, continue downhill through the next field. A deep little valley (Lime Combe) should be parallel and down to your left. You will now follow this valley all the way back to the road. In due course you will see Limecombe Cottage on the far side of the valley. Continue south, but do not turn where you see a footpath signpost pointing back, and down to the left. That track leads to Limecombe Cottage and is not the way you want. Instead, walk on for another 200 yards and then head downhill towards the valley bottom. There in the trees you will find a signpost. The path leads you across three separate plank footbridges to the far side of the valley. Now, keeping Lime Combe down to your right, you follow the path all the way to the Barle valley. At the road turn left for the short walk back to Simonsbath.

## Places of interest nearby

In Simonsbath itself there is a picnic site, a pottery and a place where cream teas may be enjoyed. For those interested in archaeology the hillsides around are scattered with ancient sites, for example, *Cow Castle* (an Iron Age settlement), *Hangley Cleave Barrows* and various standing stones. The views towards Hartland Point, from the road to South Molton, are truly magnificent.

# Withypool
## The Royal Oak Inn

9

This pub is famous, and not just locally. It is mentioned in many a pub guide and has been the subject of newspaper articles. In 1866 R.D. Blackmore stayed here whilst writing *Lorna Doone* and in 1944 General Eisenhower visited during the months before the D-Day landings. Today, it is a popular stopping place for both motorists and walkers. At weekends it can become very crowded, especially in summer when people spill onto the terrace, where tables and chairs are set out.

In truth the Royal Oak deserves its reputation, for it is indeed a friendly, cosy, well appointed establishment. The 17th-century character has been kept, there being low ceiling beams and a wealth of exposed wood and stonework. This being hunting country the walls are adorned with antlers and stag paintings, horse and hound prints and other mementoes of the local meet. There are separate bars and children are welcome in the areas away from the serving counter.

The well stocked bar dispenses Flowers IPA and Whitbread Castle Eden Ale; on handpump is draught Lane's Traditional Farmhouse cider, and a full selection of wines is always available. The range and quality of the food is excellent, the regular menus being supplemented by daily specials chalked up on blackboards. There are sandwiches and ploughman's lunches, salads and jacket potatoes, pies and casseroles, steaks and seafood. Exmoor lamb and local game are served, as are freshly-caught fish and a selection of West Country cheeses. Vegetarians have plenty of choice too, including pasta dishes and vegetable bakes.

The Royal Oak keeps normal pub opening times.

Telephone: 0164 383 1506.

*How to get there:* Withypool lies in the very heart of the Exmoor National Park, just off the B3223, 5 miles south-east of Simonsbath and 7 miles north-west of Dulverton. Porlock is 8 miles away, over the moors to the north. The Royal Oak will be found at the eastern end of the village.

*Parking:* There is a large pub car park. Vehicles can also be left along the village street, but care should be taken not to obstruct local traffic.

*Length of the walk:* 4½ miles. OS map Landranger 181 Minehead (inn GR 847356).

*Withypool stands on the river Barle, whose valley provides superb walks in each direction. Most walkers who visit this part of Exmoor seem to undertake the route to Tarr Steps and back, following the river downstream to reach the famous clapper-style packhorse bridge. Various upland walks can also be enjoyed from Withypool, by exploring the footpaths that lead up onto the open moorland. This walk, although long, is extremely easy and pleasant. The route is to Landacre Bridge and back, upstream from Withypool. The outward journey is, mostly, by tarmac lane. The return journey is via a well worn, grassy footpath along the river Barle. Some stiles are encountered but no obstacle is difficult. Landacre Bridge is a local beauty spot, which becomes very busy in summer.*

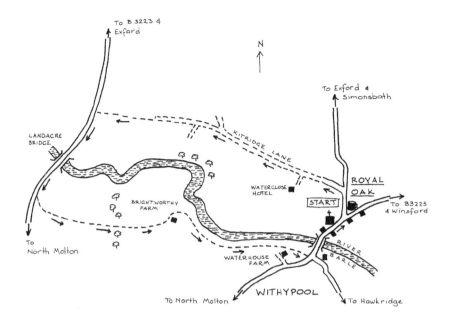

# The Walk

The outward route needs little description, being very straight and very clear. Turn right, up the road behind the Royal Oak and then, at the edge of the village, turn left along a narrow tarmac lane. This is marked as a dead-end. A bed symbol sign also tells you that an hotel is ¼ mile up the lane. Follow this lane for more than a mile as it climbs past the entrance to Westerclose Hotel and on towards the open moorland ahead. You should notice that the width between the hedgerows is much wider than the lane itself, suggesting that this route was once more important than it is nowadays. On large scale maps it is called Kitridge Lane, but in medieval times it was the road to Simonsbath. Along much of this stretch it is, today, also followed by the Two Moors Way, a designated long distance footpath linking Lynton on Exmoor with Ivybridge on the southern edge of Dartmoor, near Plymouth.

In due course the tarmac surface suddenly ends at a gate. Go through this and continue along a clear gravel track that runs across the moorland pasture. Very soon you meet the road to Landacre Bridge. Turn left and walk downhill to reach this well known beauty spot. The landscape all around is open moorland, where the rough pastures are given over to sheep and ponies. The Barle river flows attractively through this treeless valley – the five-arched stone bridge here forming a perfect focal point. If the place is not too crowded then stay awhile, and dabble your feet in the clear water.

The footpath back to Withypool begins about 100 yards beyond the bridge on the left-hand side. A signpost marks the way. Curving left slightly the route crosses a side stream by stepping-stones and proceeds to climb the grassy hillside at an angle. It then levels off and runs eastward, parallel to the river that flows down below on the left. At the line of trees, which follows a hedgebank up the valley side, you will find a signpost and gate. Continue onward, in the direction of a yellow arrow which is painted on the post to show the way. There should be no difficulty in route finding. A gravel path leads down the edge of a number of fields, eventually reaching Brightworthy Farm. Here you bear left, over a wooden bridge, and then right. The path takes you behind the farm buildings and then diagonally across a field. Thereafter, the route leads down to the river Barle itself and you accompany the waters as they bubble downstream. This is a lovely stretch and should not be rushed.

The last ½ mile involves a walk across the meadows. Round the next bend in the river you follow a wooden paddock fence to a stile in the corner of a field. Thereafter, another stile, on the left, takes you diagonally across the field below Waterhouse Farm to the flat pastures beyond. Withypool Bridge will soon be reached. Cross this and bear right for the Royal Oak.

## Places of interest nearby

There are some lovely villages hereabouts, each one old, pretty and well worth a visit. *Exford* (2 miles north) is the headquarters of the Exmoor Hunt and contains the stables and kennels necessary for the well trained animals employed. *Winsford* (4 miles east) boasts seven bridges, numerous thatched cottages and was the birthplace of Ernest Bevin, Labour politician of the post-war years.

# ⑩ Brompton Regis
## The George

Brompton Regis stands close to Wimbleball Lake, so the George attracts good custom from the sailing and angling fraternities. Walkers, coming down from nearby Haddon Hill, or from the Brendons, also tend to congregate here. All these customers should not be disappointed, since this is an excellent pub. The welcome is friendly, the atmosphere cosy and the food and drink served is delicious.

Inside, there is one main bar but one end of this is so separately positioned behind a half-wall that it acts as an intimate lounge. This is where families tend to congregate. There are beams and old fire-places but the overall character is neither dark nor antiquated. The large Georgian-style windows look out across the beer garden, beyond which is a view towards Haddon Hill. All is light and airy.

Wadworth 6X and King and Barnes Twelve Bore Bitter are the real ales available, whereas the choice of cider is Dry Blackthorn. There is also a full range of wines. But it is the wholesome, home-made and varied choice of food on offer that especially attracts the customers.

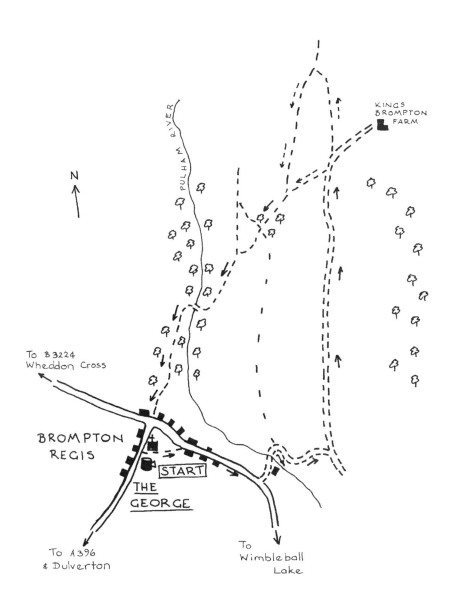

N ↑

PULHAM RIVER

KINGS
BROMPTON
FARM

To B3224
Wheddon Cross

BROMPTON
REGIS

START

THE
GEORGE

To A396
& Dulverton

To
Wimbleball
Lake

There are bar snacks like sandwiches and salads, light dishes like soups and items with chips, and main meals like steaks and fish dishes. Daily specials supplement the regular items and there are always meals suitable for vegetarians, for example, pasta bakes or vegetable and cheese dishes. The traditional desserts, like treacle pie, are always very popular.

Normal pub opening times are kept.

Telephone: 01398 371273.

*How to get there:* Brompton Regis stands in the south-east corner of the Exmoor National Park, just 4 miles north-east of Dulverton. It lies 2 miles east of the A396 Exe valley road. The George will be found next to the church.

*Parking:* There is a pub car park. Elsewhere in the village there are few places where vehicles can be left, the lanes here being narrow.

*Length of the walk:* 2½ miles (3½ miles longer option). OS map Landranger 181 Minehead (inn GR 951314).

*There are many walks to be enjoyed from Brompton Regis. Numerous footpaths link the village to Wimbleball Lake, and the lanes to the south lead to the Haddeo valley where a good riverside path passes through the woods to the village of Bury. Energetic walkers may also like to climb nearby Haddon Hill which affords fine views. This short walk, instead, takes in the pleasant hill country north of Brompton Regis. The outward journey climbs a hill spur by way of a tarmac lane; the return ramble descends by footpath along the beautiful Pulham valley. The route is clearly marked throughout. Some stiles are encountered and one short stretch runs along a grassy slope, but there is nothing that should cause any walking problems.*

**The Walk**

Take the tarmac path that leads down between the George and the churchyard, and then walk through the bottom (eastern) end of the village past the tearooms and Methodist chapel. At the edge of the village, immediately before the end-of-speed-limit signs, turn left along a tarmac lane. This takes you past a cottage, over a ford (where there is also a footbridge), and then uphill along a gravel track rutted

51

*Wimbleball Lake.*

by tractor wheels. This track climbs steeply, swings sharp right and then, after a while, bears left. At the top, where the gradient begins to level off, you meet another track, this one being much wider and firmer, surfaced with tarmac. Turn left and follow this clear track as it climbs steadily uphill. Be sure to look behind along this next stretch, for the views back towards Haddon Hill begin to open out.

You keep to this track for about a mile. After a while the gradient levels off and, round to the right, you will be able to glimpse Wimbleball Lake, between a fold of the hills. In due course, after the track has curved left, then right a bit, you reach a gate (which is usually left open). At this point – where the tarmac track bears right to go down to King's Brompton Farm – you have a choice of routes. Those wishing to lengthen their circuit by about a mile should continue straight on, beside the hedgerow, and then after crossing two large fields, turn sharp left to follow a path southwards marked by yellow-painted signs. Those wishing to keep the walk to its originally intended length should go through the first gate on the left and walk back across the field diagonally to the bottom corner, where they should continue through the gate on the right (not the one in the absolute corner).

Beyond that gate the two optional routes rejoin. From there continue diagonally, aiming for the wooded valley below. This is the Pulham valley and will lead you all the way back to Brompton Regis. In the bottom corner, amongst some trees, a stile will be found, together with a footpath signpost and a yellow-topped post. From here the route is well marked and easy to follow. Ignoring the farm tracks cutting across the route, continue along the upper slopes of the Pulham valley. At first you contour but – beyond a large boulder where a yellow-painted marker points the way – you descend gradually towards the river. If the ground is wet take care along this stretch since you are walking across sloping grassland. Down by the trees a yellow-topped post shows the way. The path crosses the river by a footbridge and continues down the valley on the other side. Brompton Regis is soon reached and the George awaits.

## Places of interest nearby

*Wimbleball Lake*, a reservoir created in the 1970s, has opportunities for fishing, sailing and rowing. There are campsites, car parks, public conveniences and nature trails. South of Brompton Regis there are two small towns well worth visiting; *Dulverton* with its old buildings and craft shops, and *Bampton* with its old castle remains and regular floral displays.

# ⑪ Minehead
## The Red Lion

Minehead is a much prettier town than some people may imagine. Away from the caravans, the amusement arcades and the Holiday Centre, there is much to appreciate. The little harbour still bustles with boats and Higher Town, on the hillside above, boasts some old and very attractive thatched cottages.

The building occupied by the Red Lion, down on the sea front, is large but not especially old, being early 20th century. But there has been a pub called the Red Lion on this site at least since the early 17th century. Sadly the original thatched building was demolished towards the end of the 19th century, having been severely damaged by storms. But what the Red Lion may lack in architecture, it more than makes up for in its friendliness, hospitality and welcome, in its wide range of food and drink, and in its opening times (normal pub opening hours being extended to all day during the holiday season). Children are welcome inside and out.

The real ales served include Courage Directors, Ruddles Best and John Smith's Bitter, as well as an intriguing 'house bitter' known as

Lions Blood. Draught ciders include Taunton Farmhouse and Rich's, and there is a full wine list. The menu is extensive and ranges from sandwiches, jacket potatoes, salads and ploughman's lunches to steaks, pies, fish dishes and curries. Children have their own menu and vegetarians are offered an excellent selection, including cheese and vegetable bakes and the tempting nutty Stilton and mushroom pie. The sweets include old favourites such as syrup pudding and spotted dick plus ices and cream cakes. All the food is home-made and reasonably priced.

Telephone: 01643 706507.

*How to get there:* Minehead stands on the north-eastern corner of the Exmoor National Park, in the shelter of that mass of upland comprising North Hill and Selworthy Beacon. The A39 trunk road now skirts around the back of town, on its way from Williton to Porlock. The Red Lion stands in Quay Street, which links the Esplanade with the harbour.

*Parking:* There is a pub car park. Elsewhere in Minehead free parking may be difficult in the height of season, there being pay meters almost everywhere. However, Blenheim Road, round the corner from the Red Lion, may offer some possibilities.

*Length of the walk:* 4 miles (shorter and longer options). OS map Landranger 181 Minehead (inn GR 971466).

*The upland area immediately west of Minehead offers splendid opportunities for circular walks. Much of the coastline is owned by the National Trust and most of the hilltop has 'access land' status allowing walkers to explore almost at will (provided, of course, the country code is observed). The paths are clear, the ground underfoot is firm and the views are wonderful. This circuit includes the summit of Bratton Ball (reached by way of the South West Coast Path) and the remains of Burgundy Chapel. The steep descent to the latter can be missed by those wishing to take an easier route back to Minehead.*

## The Walk

A short way from the Red Lion, towards the harbour, a signpost points the way left, along an alleyway between cottages that leads to a rough flight of steps. This sign states 'Start of South West Coast

55

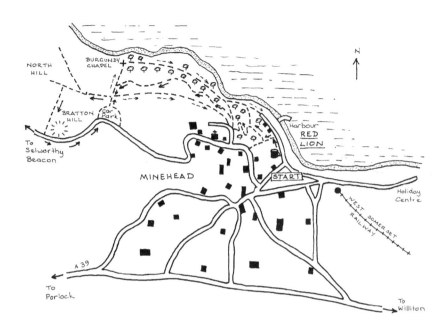

Footpath to Poole (Dorset) 500 miles'. Another signpost also tells you that the path goes to 'North Hill, St Michael's Church and Church Steps'. So begins the walk, with your appetite sufficiently whetted. In fact, the path in question – to North Hill – leads off to the right halfway up the steps. A large notice board here gives details of the South West Coast footpath, together with a map of the entire route. A future project for the dedicated walker!

The way is clear. Follow the tarmac path as it climbs steeply through the trees and zigzags up the cliff above the harbour. Towards the top of this initial ascent you reach Beacon Road, where you turn right, to follow the lane marked as a dead-end for vehicles. Soon you reach the Exmoor National Park boundary sign. Continue along the wide gravel track that runs ahead, past the sign pointing to North Hill. The climb is now constant. Ignoring other trackways, keep to the path uphill with the sea all the time on your right-hand side. Take your time and enjoy the scenery. At first you climb through the trees, but soon you emerge into the open, to walk across the heather-clad moorland that covers the clifftop. On clear days you can see the mountains of Wales – the Brecon Beacons on the misty skyline.

In due course you reach a signpost pointing to the right and indicating the Burgundy Chapel. The steep descent to that ruin begins here and those intending to undertake that stretch will later return to this spot. The path to the summit swings left to climb to another footpath signpost. This one is many-armed; the seafront and Minehead's Higher Town to the left, Woodcombe straight on, Selworthy and Bossington to the right. Follow the last. Bratton Ball summit, marked by an old concrete triangulation point, will be reached by turning left along a grassy track soon after passing a path to the coast on the right (leading to a 'rugged alternative' path). From the top, over 800 feet above sea level, the panorama is superb. Inland, the hills of Exmoor stretch to the greeny-blue yonder.

The return begins back at the many-armed footpath signpost, most easily reached down the tarmac road, bearing left across the moorland car park at the point where the road swings right as it descends. Those wishing to take the easy and short way back should follow the way marked as 'Sea Front via Coast'. The energetic and more adventurous should descend to the Burgundy Chapel signpost and continue seawards. This steep slope should not be attempted when conditions are damp and slippery. All that remains of the Burgundy Chapel is an arch and some low stone walls amid the bracken. It is medieval in date and some say it was built as a hermitage. It is certainly in a remote spot, perched alone on the low clifftop.

The path back to Minehead from the Chapel is direct. It contours along the lower cliff through bracken and woods. Beyond Greenaleigh Farm, follow the clear track, taking the lower left-hand fork whenever a choice of routes presents itself. In due course you emerge down by the beach, to walk along a tarmac path over the grassy undercliff. At the far end is Minehead harbour and, beyond, the Red Lion.

**Places of interest nearby**

*Minehead* itself has all manner of tourist attractions and children of all ages will be kept amused for hours. Those searching for quieter surroundings may like to visit *Selworthy*, an unspoilt, thatched village owned by the National Trust. It stands near the coast towards Porlock. In the other direction, eastwards, the medieval village of *Dunster* should be seen.

# 12 Washford
## The White Horse Inn

Standing on the eastern edge of the Exmoor National Park, Washford is a village much visited by tourists. Located on the West Somerset Railway Line, it boasts a railway museum devoted to the old Somerset and Dorset Line and is situated close to the Tropiquaria, an exotic wildlife centre housed in a former radio station. In addition, the grand monastic ruins of Cleeve Abbey will be found nearby.

The White Horse Inn is close to Cleeve Abbey. It is an old place, attractive both inside and out. There are low ceilings, bare stone walls and – during winter months – two open fires. The beer garden, like the car park, is across the road, on the far side of the Washford river. There is a weir nearby, and an old mill, so the prospect is very pleasant indeed. What a pity the place is open only during normal pub opening times!

This is a friendly pub where the food is good and reasonably priced, the choice of drinks wide-ranging and the décor comfortable and homely. Children are welcome. There is one large bar room, with a pool and darts area at one end, and a section set aside for dining.

The real ales served include Ruddles County, Ushers Best and Webster's Yorkshire, while cider drinkers will find Red Rock and a local farmhouse brew on draught. Apart from daily specials, which are written up on the blackboard, there is a regular menu offering a selection that should suit everyone, even vegetarians. Choices range from sandwiches, ploughman's lunches, jacket potatoes and omelettes to things with chips, pasta dishes and cheese-based bakes, as well as main meals like meat pies, chicken meals and various fish dishes.

Telephone: 01984 640415.

*How to get there:* Washford lies on the A39, 2 miles inland from Watchet and 6 miles south-east of Minehead. The Brendon Hills, which form the eastern end of the Exmoor National Park, rise up on the landward side. The White Horse Inn stands in the hamlet of Hungerford, ½ mile south of Washford.

*Parking:* There is a large pub car park. Vehicles may also be left some 300 yards away, in a public car park opposite Cleeve Abbey.

*Length of the walk:* 3½ miles (3 mile shorter option). OS map Landranger 181 Minehead (inn GR 046402).

*There are many pleasant walks from Washford. One of these follows the route of an old mineral railway line down the valley to Watchet; another uses footpaths and lanes to reach Nettlecombe and the hills above Monksilver. The walk described here leads up one side of the Washford valley, and returns down the other side. Two pleasant little villages are visited, Roadwater and Torre, and the views throughout are extremely attractive. The route is very easy to follow, keeping to clear footpaths and trackways on the outward journey and returning along narrow country lanes. There are a few stiles to climb, but these should not be a problem.*

## The Walk

The first stretch requires a short road walk, north to Washford village. On the way you pass Cleeve Abbey and those with time may like to visit this splendidly preserved monastic complex. Now run by English Heritage, the site contains an almost complete gatehouse and various cloister buildings, including a dining hall still protected by a magni-

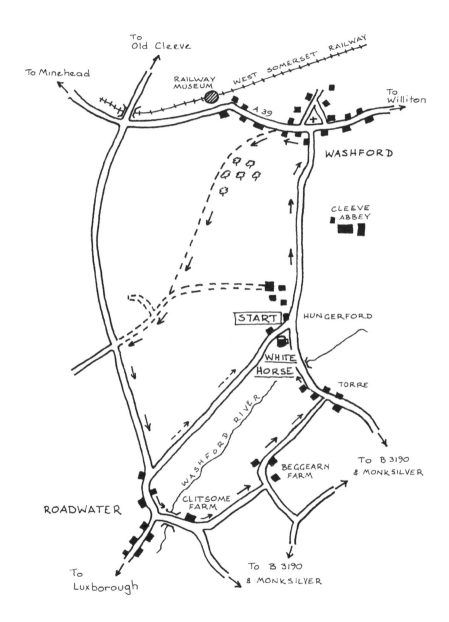

ficent 15th-century roof. In medieval times the Abbey was run by the austere Cistercian order of monks. An exhibition explains the details of their daily life.

Upon reaching the busy A39 road, at Washford village, you turn left. Fortunately you do not remain on this trunk road for long. After just 200 yards bear left, taking a track that leads behind a petrol filling station. This track soon ends abruptly at a gate, beyond which are open fields. But the footpath continues. Climb the stile next to the gate and follow the top edge of the field as it climbs towards the corner of a woodland. There, another stile leads you onwards, beside that woodland. The route actually needs little description. It is fairly straight and follows the top edges of a number of fields. The stiles between each field have arrow discs showing the way. All along this stretch the views are superb. To the right and behind is the sea and the coast towards Minehead; straight on are the tree-clad slopes of the Brendon Hills. Down below, back in the Washford direction, you may see and hear the steam trains as they chug their way along the West Somerset Railway line. The engines run all year round but are especially frequent during holiday times.

In due course, the path is joined by a gravel track that comes up from the left. Continue straight on along this track. Soon afterwards ignore another track as it leads off to the right. Continue in the same direction as before. Soon you reach the road. Turn left and go steeply downhill to the village of Roadwater. (Those wishing to shorten the circuit by ½ mile may turn left again at the edge of the village, taking the road along the western side of the valley.) Roadwater is a long and narrow settlement running along the bottom of the Washford river valley. If time permits, explore a little, and notice the few remaining signs that this was once an industrial village, situated alongside a mineral railway line. Iron ore was carried this way during the 19th century, from Goosemoor (on top of the Brendon Hills) to Watchet harbour.

The little country lane that will take you back to the White Horse Inn begins at a thatched cottage called 'Riverside', at the northern end of Roadwater. Walk over the bridge and turn left after Clitsome Farm. The lane then rises steeply, under the trees, before levelling off. For nearly a mile you keep to this lane, turning left at the junction near Beggearn Huish, and left again at the hamlet of Torre. But it is not a busy road. It is narrow and hemmed in by earthy hedgebanks. Indeed, so quiet is it that grass almost grows down the middle.

*Cleeve Abbey.*

## Places of interest nearby

Apart from the attractions already mentioned in Washford, there is *Combe Sydenham Country Park* near Monksilver, *Home Farm* at Blue Anchor (a working farm with a children's play area), and *Bee World and Animal Centre* near Stogumber. *Dunster* should not be missed with its Castle owned by the National Trust, and *Watchet* boasts a bustling harbour still very much in commercial use.

# 13 Frithelstock
## The Clinton Arms

Frithelstock is a small, hilltop village overlooking attractive Devon countryside, across the Torridge valley. There are some old cottages here and an interesting church. But visitors come here for two par-ticular reasons. One of these is to see the beautiful ruins of a priory, which dates from the 13th century. The other is to sample the splendid food cooked at the Clinton Arms.

To say that some of the daily specials here are unusual is to make an understatement. Wild boar, kangaroo, ostrich, bison, crocodile and peacock are just some of the items that might be offered. By comparison, such dishes as Stilton and spinach tagliatelle and mushroom stroganoff seem almost mundane! Not that other, more normal, items are excluded. There are also sandwiches, jacket pota-toes, omelettes, fish and seafood courses and meat pies to tempt the customers. So there is plenty of choice even for the less adventurous. To wash your meal down there are real ales, such as Bass and a guest beer like Tetley, draught Gaymers Olde English cider and numerous wines.

Inside – and apart from the restaurant – there is just one low beamed bar, which is decorated in traditional style. Beyond this there is a small snug area and a room with a pool table. Outside is a small garden at the back (with children's play equipment) and an open area in front where tables are laid out. The welcome is very friendly and the service very good. There must be many satisfied customers here. The Clinton Arms keeps to normal pub opening times. Telephone: 01805 623279.

*How to get there:* Frithelstock stands just off the A386, 2 miles west of Great Torrington and 5 miles south of Bideford. The Clinton Arms faces the village green, opposite the church.

*Parking:* There is a pub car park and some space for vehicles on the gravel that surrounds the village green. Cars should not be left along the side of the road, this being narrow, but there is a large layby some 400 yards to the east.

*Length of the walk:* 4 miles. OS map Landranger 180 Barnstaple and Ilfracombe (inn GR 464194).

*There are many good walks to enjoy around Great Torrington and the tourist office issues some excellent leaflets detailing their routes. The valley of the river Torridge, in this area, is steep-sided and wooded, affording some excellent views. This circuit includes a length of the Tarka Trail, a long distance footpath designated by Devon County Council. It links the Exmoor coast with Dartmoor and wanders through the scenery made famous by Henry Williamson in his book* Tarka the Otter. *To reach the Tarka Trail, footpaths across farmland are used, to return from it a trackway and lane are used. Some steep gradients are involved.*

**The Walk**
Turn left outside the Clinton Arms and proceed along the road as it winds and descends away from the village. Beyond the house called Southview you reach the last, isolated, cottage on the left. Immediately before this house turn left, through the gate, and walk up over the field. A footpath signpost points the way. In fact, there is no apparent path or track but the route is certainly a right of way. It runs almost due south, across a small valley, to a farmstead called Pryston.

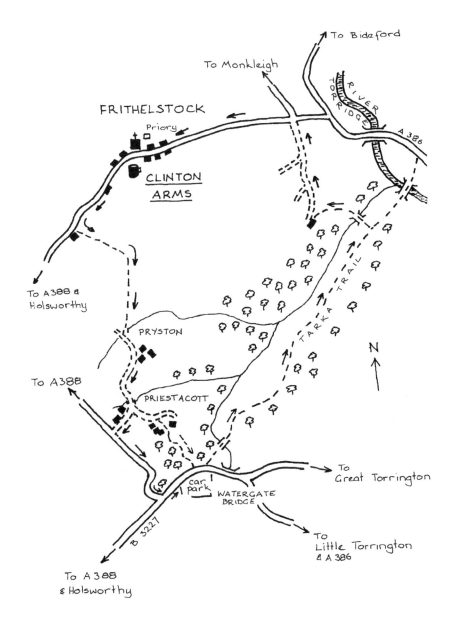

To Bideford

To Monkleigh

RIVER TORRIDGE

A 386

FRITHELSTOCK

Priory

CLINTON
ARMS

TARKA TRAIL

To A388 &
Holsworthy

PRYSTON

N

To A388

PRIESTACOTT

To
Great Torrington

To A388

car
park

WATERGATE
BRIDGE

To
Little Torrington
& A 386

B 3227

To A388
& Holsworthy

Having walked up to the skyline and on to a gate on the far side of the first field, continue into the next field. Bearing half-right cross diagonally down to the far corner. There, amongst the bushes at the valley bottom, a gate leads you onto a gravel track. Follow this up to the farmstead.

Respecting the privacy of the farmstead inhabitants you skirt the edge of the buildings, keeping to the gravel track that runs around the western side. Continue along the concrete track beyond. In due course, this becomes a tarmac track and bends left to reach another group of buildings called, on the map, Priestacott. Here you have a choice of routes. The longer, but easier, way is to continue through this settlement to reach the road and then turn left to join the B3227, where you turn left again. The shorter, but harder, way is to keep left along a grassy track where the tarmac track bends right. This brings you to another farmstead, where stands a large thatched cottage. From here an overgrown footpath leads downhill through fields and woods. Both routes end at Watergate Bridge where there is a Tarka Trail car park and information board.

The Tarka Trail, heading north from Watergate Bridge, offers a splendid walk. It follows a deeply-cut wooded valley, following the course of a now disused railway line. The ground underfoot is firm, being rolled gravel. It is also a popular cycle track, and at intervals along its length wooden seats are provided. For about 1½ miles you can enjoy the sights and sounds of the valley; the branches above and the river below.

In due course you reach a point where a gate straddles the Tarka Trail path (to discourage vehicular traffic). Here a public bridleway signpost points left. Follow this direction to walk through a side gate, over a bridge and then, half-left, across a grassy meadow. Along by some trees go through the next gate, on the left, and head back towards a cottage, half-hidden in the wood. Upon reaching that cottage, strike back to the right and up a stony track. This climbs steadily beneath the trees. Ignoring other tracks, which join from the left, keep to this main trackway, eventually reaching a road. Turn left, and climb steeply for about ½ mile back to Frithelstock.

## Places of interest nearby

Great Torrington has many attractions, but the two most famous are the *Rosemoor Garden* and the *Dartington Crystal Factory*. The former is owned by the Royal Horticultural Society and offers colour and interest all year round. The latter gives glass-making demonstrations and contains a shop where many fine items can be purchased.

# ⑭ Dolton
## The Royal Oak

Dolton is a pretty place, with many thatched cottages, but it seems too small to have three inns. However, all three are excellent, being cosy, traditional and well appointed. They are all popular and all serve a wide range of food and drink. The Rams Head and Union Inn are situated on the main road, the Royal Oak stands in the old village square. It is the last which seems to be the oldest of the three. It is said that the Royal Oak dates back to the beginning of the 16th century and stands on earlier foundations. Inside, the character of the building has been maintained well, there being low ceiling beams, a stone fireplace and floors at different levels. To the left as you enter is a restaurant and to your right is the lounge bar. Behind the latter is a small snug area and, beyond that, a large public bar with pool table.

Furgusons Dartmoor Best Bitter is the regular real ale available on draught, together with a changing guest beer, a traditional scrumpy cider (Inch's Stonehouse) and a good selection of wines. A regular menu – which includes rolls, salads, pies and items with chips – is supplemented by daily specials. These may include steak and kidney

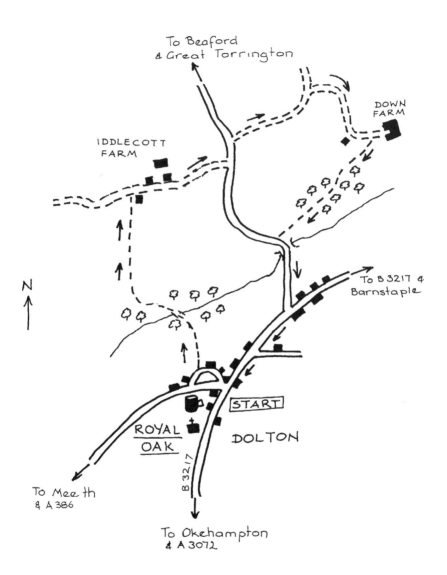

To Beaford
& Great Torrington

DOWN
FARM

IDDLECOTT
FARM

To B 3217 &
Barnstaple

N

START

ROYAL
OAK

DOLTON

B 3217

To Meeth
& A 386

To Okehampton
& A 3072

pie, salmon and various 'exotic' dishes like pasta bakes and curries. Amongst the desserts the sticky toffee pudding is especially popular. The Royal Oak does not have a ghost as such, but locals say that it does have a ghostly smell. On winter evenings the aroma of smoked ham wafts along the passageways, even when the kitchen is closed!

A warm welcome awaits you at the Royal Oak, which keeps to normal pub opening times.

Telephone: 01805 804288.

*How to get there:* Dolton stands on the B3217 road, which winds its way from Okehampton in the south to the Taw Valley, near Barnstaple, in the north. This is not a well known part of Devon. Great Torrington is 6 miles north-west, and Winkleigh is 5 miles south-east. The Royal Oak is close to the church.

*Parking:* The village square, in front of the Royal Oak, acts as the pub car park. Elsewhere in Dolton vehicles can be left by the road-sides, provided no obstruction is caused.

*Length of the walk:* 2 miles. OS map Landranger 180 Barnstaple and Ilfracombe (inn GR 570121).

*Dolton stands on the edge of the Torridge valley, along which there are many opportunities for good walks. Less than 2 miles away, south of Beaford, is a nature reserve. The Tarka Trail long distance footpath, from the Exmoor coast to Dartmoor, runs nearby and this offers a splendid walk in both directions, along the route of an old railway line. This circular walk wanders around a little tributary valley of the river Torridge. The route is clear throughout, using farmland paths and farm tracks. The views are pleasant and, on clear days, the Dartmoor skyline can be seen.*

## The Walk

The route begins opposite the front entrance to the Royal Oak, down a lane between two thatched cottages. A footpath signpost points the way. At the bungalow called Meadowcroft, keep to the left and cross over the stile you see in front. This leads to a path that goes downhill, through horse paddocks, to the wooded combe ahead. At the bottom corner, amongst the trees, another stile takes you to a footbridge. On the far side of the stream continue along the woodland path that curves left. At the edge of the trees a third stile brings you out into the open, where you turn right.

At first you follow a clear grassy track that runs uphill, but soon this track seems to disappear into the field. Continue to climb up the valley side, keeping the hedgerow to your right. At the top, next to some corrugated iron barns, a gate leads onto a main gravel trackway. Turn right, walk through the farmyard and then along the concrete and tarmac lane to the road, passing an attractive farm pond on your way. At the road turn left and then, very shortly, right along another gravel trackway. This one leads to Down Farm and is signposted as a footpath.

This track (which later becomes concrete-surfaced) bends left, then right, then right again in order to reach the farm. A good view of Dartmoor, on the distant skyline, may be enjoyed in fine weather. Towards the end of this track there is a bungalow, beyond which a sharp left bend heads for the main farmstead. At this bend, however, go through the gate ahead and bear right across the field. An arrow disc points the way. Descend diagonally to the bottom corner where another gate will be found. Through this (or over it, should it prove difficult to open) continue along the top edge of a small woodland. Soon the path dips slightly, to run beneath the trees. This is an attractive stretch and should not be rushed.

Beyond another gate continue in the same direction, by now leaving the woodland behind. Keep the stream down to the left as you walk over the rough grassland that covers the gentle valley side. Amongst the distant trees you will find a gate and stile, on the far side of which is the road. Turn left uphill along that road and right at the junction at the top. The Royal Oak will be reached up Fore Street.

## Places of interest nearby

At Merton (3 miles west), is *Barometer World* where antique barometers are displayed and visitors can see all manner of barometric items being made and repaired. Just 2 miles south-east is the privately owned *Stafford Moor Fishery* where a series of lakes, and a tackle shop, are a must for dedicated anglers. *Hatherleigh* (6 miles south) is a pretty old town situated on the edge of a moorland landscape well known for its wildlife.

# South Molton
## 15 The Tiverton Inn

South Molton is an attractive, bustling town which remains, very much, the market centre for an agricultural community. There are numerous old buildings, including a 14th-century church, an 18th-century Guildhall and many interesting shops, craft centres, restaurants and inns.

The Tiverton Inn must be one of the most pleasant of the inns here, being friendly, traditional and well appointed. Children are welcome and an excellent range of food and drink is offered. There is one large bar room but this extends, on each side, back beyond the bar counter. To the right is the area with the pool table and to the left is the almost separate dining room. Everywhere there are low ceiling beams, and pictures of old South Molton adorn the walls. At one end is a large stone fireplace, used in winter to make the pub especially cosy.

Whitbread Castle Eden Ale and Brakspear Bitter are the real ales available, together with Strongbow cider and a selection of wines, including a good house red. But it is the food here that tempts in the

71

customers. A regular menu, plus daily specials, offer everything that anyone could wish for, including items for vegetarians. Apart from such bar snacks as sandwiches and jacket potatoes, there are main meals that include steaks, pies, fish and pasta dishes. From the traditional (steak and kidney pie) to the foreign (various curries), and from the homely (cottage pie) to the unusual (nut roast) the choice is sure to please.

Normal pub opening times are kept.

Telephone: 01769 572525.

*How to get there:* South Molton stands just a few miles south of the Exmoor National Park, on the banks of the river Mole, a tributary of the river Taw. It is very close to the A361 that links Tiverton and Barnstaple, these towns being 18 and 10 miles away respectively. The Tiverton Inn stands near the town centre, in East Street, now the B3227 but once the main Tiverton road.

*Parking:* This being a town centre pub, there is no pub car park. However, there are many places in town where cars may be left. The side streets, generally, are not busy and there is a large public car park to the south of the town centre, in Mill Street.

*Length of the walk:* 4 miles. OS map Landranger 180 Barnstaple and Ilfracombe (inn GR 716259).

*This may be slightly long, for a 'short' walk, but it is very easy. Almost the entire length is along country lanes and gravel trackways. The only stretch which follows a footpath runs along a river bank, through a delightfully attractive woodland. There are some gradients to negotiate but nothing is very steep. All the views are pleasantly rural, across the Mole valley.*

## The Walk

This circuit crosses the countryside south of South Molton, so it is perhaps fitting that it should begin down South Street. This leads down from the far end of the town centre, as approached from the Tiverton Inn. Broad Street acts as the town's nucleus and time should be spent wandering about its immediate surroundings. The church stands up a tree-lined path to the north, the covered Market Hall stands opposite, to the south. The latter – more accurately called the

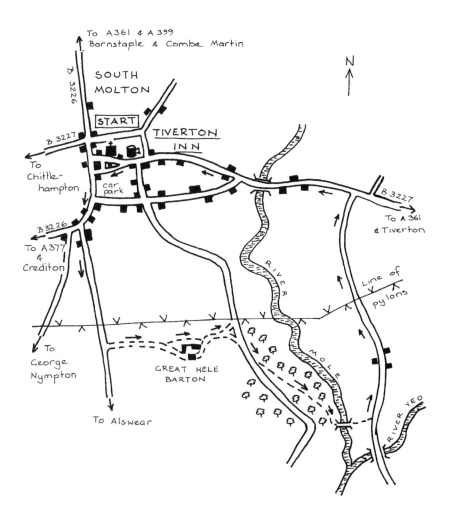

Pannier Market – was built in the 19th century and is used by stall-holders on Thursdays and Saturdays. Walk down South Street to the edge of town, at which point it bears right. Here, turn left down the lane signposted to the Community College and Sports Hall. Do *not* go down the lane signposted to George Nympton which leads off close by. The lane required is called, on the town plan, Old Alswear Road.

Continue southwards, past the last of the houses, and out into open countryside. Soon after the line of pylons turn left down a tarmac track. This is marked as an approach road to Great Hele Barton, but it is also a public footpath, as a signpost indicates. When you reach Great Hele Barton, however, you leave the track. In order to give the owners of this farmstead some privacy the public right of way skirts the northern edge of the buildings. So, keeping the barns to your right, continue along a field edge and then through a farm gate. Beyond this you can rejoin the tarmac track. Continue eastwards until you reach the B3137 and turn right.

Fortunately you need only walk along this road for about 300 yards. After the first bend take the footpath signposted on the left-hand side. Some concrete steps lead down and the path descends at an angle through the woodland. It is a very clear, well worn path and offers a very pretty walk beneath the trees. Ignoring other tracks to the left and right, follow the main path down towards the river, which flows at the bottom of the slope. In due course you have to climb a stile and, shortly after this, you emerge into the open. Walk across the meadow, over a footbridge and continue up to the road, where another stile awaits.

Once onto the road turn left, and remain on the road for almost a mile. It is very quiet and you will be most unlucky to meet a moving vehicle. It climbs past a couple of farmsteads and then levels off, to give some views north, towards North Molton. Despite the line of pylons, which you walk under for the second time, the prospect is very pretty. At the main road (the B3227) turn left to reach South Molton. There is a pavement all the way back to the Tiverton Inn.

**Places of interest nearby**
Apart from a small and interesting museum, South Molton also boasts the *Quince Honey Farm* (at the edge of town on the Barnstaple road). Here the 'Indoor Apiary' and glass booths allow visitors to see the work of honey bees. Produce is also sold at the farm shop. On the B3226, at Clapworthy 3 miles away, is *Hancocks Devon Cider Mill*, where visitors can see traditional 'scrumpy' made. Further away, near Chittlehampton, is the *Cobbaton Combat Collection*, a museum of old armoured vehicles.

# ⑯ Knowstone
## The Masons Arms Inn

Most of Knowstone village has been designated a conservation area, and this is not surprising, as it is quiet, pretty and old. Many of the buildings, like the Masons Arms itself, are thatched and date from the early Middle Ages. In fact, the Masons Arms seems to have kept much of its medieval character. The rooms are small and dark, with low beamed ceilings and flagstone floors. The half-planked walls and timberwork are hung with old farm implements, bottles and tankards, the seats are settles, and the large inglenook fireplace contains an old bread oven. In short, the place is wonderfully evocative of the English tavern at its best. No wonder it is both popular and famous.

Real ales like Hall and Woodhouse Badger Best and Cotleigh Tawny are drawn straight from the cask. Inch's and Stonehouse draught ciders and a good selection of wines are also available. But it is the excellent range and quality of the food on offer that brings customers back. Bar snacks include ploughman's lunches with a choice of West Country cheeses, various salads and home-made pies; main meals include steaks, curries and fish dishes; desserts range from ice-creams to traditional English puddings. Daily specials are written up on blackboards and there is always a good choice for vegetarians, such as pasta or vegetable bakes. The set-price evening menu offers good value and the restaurant is frequently full.

The Masons Arms, which keeps normal pub opening times, is a friendly, welcoming place that should not be missed.

Telephone: 01398 341231.

*How to get there:* Knowstone stands just a mile north of the A361, between South Molton (7 miles east) and Tiverton (10 miles north-west), and 4 miles south of the Exmoor National Park boundary. The Masons Arms will be found at the eastern end of the village, opposite the church.

*Parking:* There is a pub car park and vehicles can also be left on the opposite side of the road, in front of the churchyard wall. Elsewhere in the village parking space is limited owing to the narrowness of the lanes.

*Length of the walk:* 2½ miles (2 mile shorter option). OS map Landranger 181 Minehead (inn GR 828231).

*Knowstone stands on the edge of a moorland area, across which are many fine walks. The village is also a popular stopping point for those undertaking the Two Moors Way long distance footpath. Knowstone Moor is an upland region of bracken and gorse and affords fine views towards Exmoor and Dartmoor. This circuit, however, offers a pretty alternative to a moorland walk. It follows the valley of the Crooked Oak river, downstream to an area of woodland. The footpaths used are all clear, being generally well worn. A few stiles are encountered, and some fairly steep gradients, but no part of the walk is difficult. The views, throughout, are very pleasant, across rolling farmland, bracken-clad slopes and wooded combes.*

## The Walk

The footpath begins just yards away from the Masons Arms, next to a thatched cottage called Enfield. This will be found west of the pub, so turn right as you leave the bar room door. A wooden gate leads you through to a private garden. Respecting the privacy of the owners, go straight over to the stile on the far side, and then continue across the

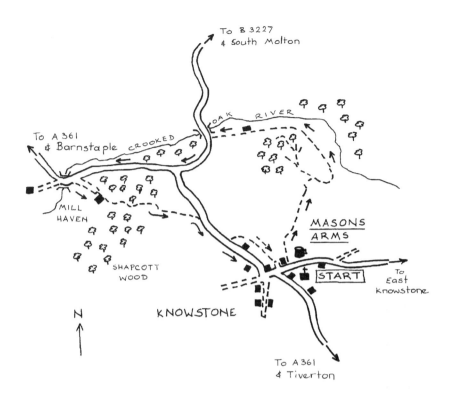

To B 3227
& South Molton

OAK RIVER

To A 361
& Barnstaple    CROOKED

MILL
HAVEN

MASONS
ARMS

SHAPCOTT
WOOD

START

To
East
Knowstone

N

KNOWSTONE

To A 361
& Tiverton

field diagonally half-right. In the bottom corner, beyond a ditch-like stream, another stile leads you through to the next field. Following the direction indicated by the yellow arrow disc, contour along the bottom of the valley slope keeping the hedgerow to your right. Round the corner of this field turn right through a third stile. This one may, in summer, be half-hidden by the hedgerow undergrowth. On the far side you enter an area of open land, with bracken and gorse sloping down into the valley. This is a very attractive landscape and time should be spent enjoying both the views and the wildlife.

Follow the path that leads down to the right. This curves round and proceeds to follow the valley bottom along. The Crooked Oak river is now on your right and a very attractive stream it is too. In due course you reach some old animal sheds. Beyond these you continue along the valley, following a clear trackway, until you reach a gate onto the road. Turn left to walk steeply up this road to the junction at the top. You now have a choice. To shorten the circuit by ½ mile turn left and walk back directly to Knowstone along the road. To continue with the circuit as planned, turn right and walk down the road under the trees. Soon you rejoin the Crooked Oak river which is still to your right.

Continue along the road beyond the woodland until you reach a gravel track, leading back on the left-hand side. This is signposted as a footpath, despite also being the drive to a house called Mill Haven. Walk through the private garden, behind the house, keeping strictly to the marked right of way. At the far end, a gate leads you to a path that climbs steadily through Shapcott Wood. This is a fairly steep path, leading up between the bracken, but it is clear as it wanders amongst the trees. At the top, at the woodland edge, you reach a gate and a large field. Cross diagonally this field, aiming for the top of the hill brow and then down the other side. In the far corner a stile takes you onto the road. Turn right for the short descent into the village. You can cut off a slight corner by using the footpath arrowed left, immediately beyond the 'Knowstone' sign. But either way, the Masons Arms is not far away.

## Places of interest nearby

*Knowstone Moor* is now protected by the Devon Wildlife Trust and offers good opportunities for wildlife spotting – deer, badgers and buzzards all being residents. The area also contains many ancient sites that may interest archaeologists, like burial mounds and pre-historic settlements. Of the many pretty villages around here, you should visit *Rackenford, Molland* and *East Anstey.*

# Lapford
## (17) The Old Malt Scoop Inn

Lapford is a very attractive, largely undiscovered, hilltop village, overlooking the Yeo valley. Ancient cottages cluster around the main 15th-century church and various farmsteads stand happily on the slopes below. No one knows for sure the age of the Old Malt Scoop Inn, but it is thought to be one of the oldest buildings here. Some say it was used to house the medieval craftsmen who worked on the church.

Today the Old Malt Scoop has been refurbished, but it still retains great character. Beyond the stone-floored lobby is the main bar room where low ceiling beams and an inglenook fireplace give a cosy, traditional atmosphere. There is also a separate dining room, a skittle alley and a room where the pool table stands. Pictures decorate the walls and all the furniture is suitably wooden.

The choice of drink is wide, from real ale like Theakston Best, Morland Old Speckled Hen and Wadworth 6X to draught Gaymers Olde English cider, numerous wines and Irish stouts. But the choice of food is wider still, and it is excellent quality. There are bar snacks, regular main course items and daily specials, as well as a children's menu and a separate vegetarians' menu. The varied menus include traditional English dishes and foreign concoctions; for example, salads, meals with chips, pies, curries, lasagnes and pasta bakes. Specialities might include swordfish steak with lemon and garlic sauce, or haddock with prawns and cheese.

The Old Malt Scoop is a welcoming place which generally keeps normal pub opening times. In summer months, however, it stays open for afternoon teas.

Telephone: 01363 83330.

*How to get there:* Lapford stands just off the A377 road, some 8 miles north-west of Crediton. It can also be reached from the B3042 which links Chawleigh and Witheridge. The Old Malt Scoop Inn will be found opposite the church.

*Parking:* There is a pub car park, reached through the central archway of the building. Vehicles can also be left in the village, most of the lanes being wide enough and sufficiently quiet.

*Length of the walk:* 4 miles (3½ mile shorter option). OS map Landranger 191 Okehampton (inn GR 733083).

*The countryside is lovely around Lapford and there are many trackways and lanes for walkers to enjoy, and many old hamlets and villages to explore. The Yeo valley is steeply wooded. Downstream, 3 miles away along the river Taw near Eggesford, various 'forest walks' have been designated and a picnic area has been laid out next to a car park. This circular walk crosses the Yeo valley and goes to the village of Nymet Rowland and back. Country lanes are used, together with footpaths across farmland. The route is, generally, very clear. There are, however, some stiles and gates to climb.*

## The Walk

The footpath begins just a few yards down the hill from the Old Malt Scoop Inn. It will be found on the left, at the entrance to Court Barton Farm, and starts as a concrete track running down by a wall. In due course, beyond some barns, it becomes a stony track and then, keeping right at a fork, it becomes a rutted grassy track between hedgerows. At the bottom of the slope this track swings right and

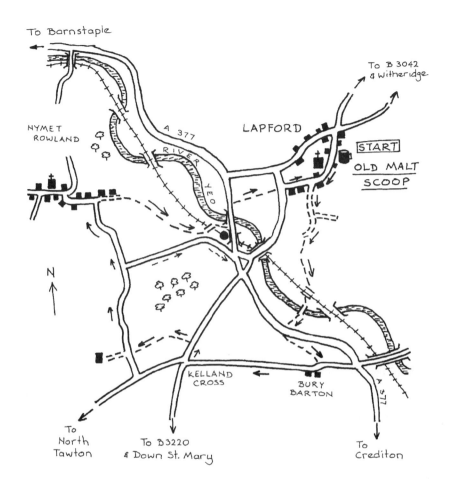

ends. At this point, go over the stile ahead and follow the direction indicated by the yellow arrow disc.

From this point you walk south across open farmland. Down in the far corner of the first field, amongst the trees, a stile leads you onwards over a little footbridge and under the railway line. Through the gate beyond, cross the next field diagonally half-left. On the far side a long, narrow footbridge takes you across the river Yeo. From here bear half-right and walk up the grassy slope to a stile and the road. Go straight over and follow the footpath opposite, following the direction indicated by the signpost. An angled ascent will bring you to another road, where you turn right. For the next ½ mile you

*The thatched medieval chapel at Bury Barton farm.*

keep to the country lane. But it is a little used lane and your walk should be very pleasant. At the first farmstead you reach (Bury Barton), notice the medieval chapel that stands forlornly amongst the barns. This backs onto the roadside.

At the junction of Kelland Cross, turn right. About 200 yards further on, turn left along the footpath signposted. This follows the edge of a field, the hedgerow being on your left. Halfway along this path, however, go through the gate which is set into this hedgerow. Proceed uphill, along the edge of the next field. This will bring you to another country lane, where you turn right. You now keep to this lane for a mile, all the way to Nymet Rowland. Those who wish to shorten their walk by ½ mile should turn right again at the first junction, reached before the village. Those with spare time should continue through the village and take a look at the church, which stands at the western end. It dates from the 15th century and boasts an oak arcade, carved to look like stone.

The return to Lapford begins at the eastern end of Nymet Rowland. Walk down the track that begins near the bungalow called Far View and ends at a farmyard. The route ahead is shown by numerous arrow discs. Continue through several gates and then along a grassy track that runs east beside a hedgerow. Lapford should be seen clearly ahead. Go through the next gate and continue along by the next hedgerow. In the following field bear half-right, descending to a stile below the trees. Thereafter, bear left to reach a gate which stands in the corner, close to the railway line. A path continues from there, beside and then over the railway line, finally to emerge by Lapford Railway Station. The return to the Old Malt Scoop is now easy. Turn left up the main road, for a short way, and then right up a gravel and tarmac path. This climbs the hill towards the village centre, through several kissing-gates.

## Places of interest nearby

Near Witheridge (7 miles north-east) is the *Southwick Country Herb Centre* which contains herb and wildflower displays, a craft centre and refreshment facilities. Near Zeal Monachorum (3 miles south) is the *Down St Mary Vineyard and Winery* which demonstrates winemaking and sells its produce.

# ⑱ Black Dog
## The Black Dog Inn

Little more than a hamlet in the middle of nowhere, Black Dog is a settlement that grew up, originally, around a pub, a cluster of farms and a crossroads. And it is the pub which remains the happy focal point. It is a friendly, welcoming establishment, popular with locals and tourists alike. The building is old and, inside, has a wealth of traditional features – low beams, settle seats, a large stone fireplace and a wood-burning stove. Everywhere, the walls are hung with horse brasses and other pieces of tackle. There is a legend of a 'Black Dog' ghost which is seen hereabouts and the local folk group, which meets regularly at the pub, annually celebrates its sightings by walking a large 'hobby horse'-style model through the nearby lanes.

Available on draught are Flowers IPA and Boddingtons real ales and Gaymers Olde English and Strongbow cider. There are also various wines on offer. But it is the food here which is especially good, with a wide range of succulent home-made dishes. Snacks include sandwiches, hot dogs, burgers and ploughman's lunches; main courses feature all manner of steaks, grills, pies and fish items.

The seafood dishes are particularly popular, including clams, mussels and prawns, whilst vegetarian options range from pancake rolls to vegetable lasagne. Such daily specials, written on the large blackboard above the mantelpiece, should satisfy everyone.

The Black Dog, which opens normal pub hours but closes some weekday lunchtimes, also has a skittle alley and a room set aside for families.

Telephone: 01884 860336.

*How to get there:* Black Dog village is set in the heart of unspoilt rural Devon, well away from any main roads, 6 miles north of Crediton and 10 miles west of Tiverton. It can most easily be reached from Witheridge, turning off the B3042 road to Chawleigh at Thelbridge. The pub will be found on the main crossroads at the village centre.

*Parking:* There is a pub car park and space is also available opposite, in a gravel layby. Vehicles may also be left along the roadsides, provided no obstruction is caused.

*Length of the walk:* 3½ miles (4½ mile longer option). OS map Landranger 191 Okehampton (inn GR 806098).

*There are footpaths all around this village, so many good walks can be enjoyed. Heading north you can reach the pretty village of Washford Pyne or the wooded valley of the river Datch, while to the south are the upper tributary streams of the river Creedy, where there is a scattering of isolated farmsteads. This walk heads east, to Woolfardisworthy. The route is clear throughout, following a trackway for most of the outward route and country lanes for the return journey. One stretch follows the bottom of an extremely pretty combe. Woolfardisworthy is an attractive small hamlet with an interesting church.*

## The Walk
Turn left outside the Black Dog pub and walk along the road, signposted to Puddington and Tiverton. Ignoring the left fork to Washford Pyne, continue to the point where a stony track leads off to the right. This is marked as the way to Higher Densham and is the route required. It bears right at a bungalow, then sharp left to reach the

85

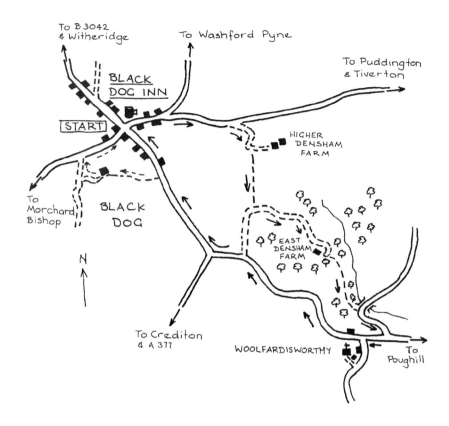

To B 3042 & Witheridge

To Washford Pyne

To Puddington & Tiverton

BLACK DOG INN

START

HIGHER DENSHAM FARM

To Morchard Bishop

BLACK DOG

N

EAST DENSHAM FARM

To Crediton & A 377

WOOLFARDISWORTHY

To Poughill

main farmstead. At this second bend go straight on, down an earthy track. This crosses a small stream, which is more like a ditch, and ends at a gate to a field. Proceed straight on.

In fact, you follow the edge of three fields, all the time keeping the hedgerow to your right-hand side. At the far end you meet a trackway once more, this one being wide and gravel surfaced. Turn left and follow this all the way to the next farmstead (East Densham). There you continue through the main yard, beside the barns, and then turn right to go through a gate. Beyond, keep to the track as it passes the farmhouse, heading downhill between hedgerows to a woodland at the bottom. Under the trees this track bends right and stops. Go through the gate on the left. Two paths present themselves on the far side. Choose the lower, left-hand one.

You now have a most delightful ½ mile walk down the bottom of a beautiful unspoilt valley. All the while keep the stream to your immediate left. The path is clear all the way, first as it wanders beneath the trees, then as it follows the edge of a field. The vegetation is rough pasture, with patches of bracken and thistle. In summer the scene is verdant, all being quiet, except for birdsong. Through the next patch of woodland the path can sometimes be a trifle damp, as it meanders through the undergrowth, but this should not spoil your enjoyment of the surroundings. Eventually you reach the road. Turn right and walk steeply uphill to a junction, where you turn right again to reach Woolfardisworthy.

Before returning to Black Dog, along the country lane heading west, you should visit the church. To do this go left at the next junction and, later, right up the track to St Mary's church. A pretty spot awaits you, complete with a thatched cottage, a medieval church and, all around, views across the Devon hills. The lane back to the pub is narrow and so quiet that grass grows along the middle in places. Take your time and enjoy the views. On clear days Dartmoor can be seen to the south. At the T-junction turn right. An optional extra mile might be enjoyed by those with the time and energy. This involves taking the footpath that leads left, a few hundred yards before the first houses of Black Dog village. This leads down to an attractive wooded combe. Up the far side of this you join a track and turn right. This will bring you back to the pub, approaching it from the west.

## Places of interest nearby

*Crediton* (6 miles away) is an interesting town with old buildings and narrow streets. In the Tourist Office you will find an excellent leaflet describing a 'town trail' that can be followed. South of Tiverton and 8 miles south-east of Black Dog is *Bickleigh*. The Castle there has a Civil War display and maritime exhibition, and Bickleigh Mill contains the 'Devonshire's Centre', which offers various tourist facilities, including a farm museum, 'birdland' and shops.

# Holcombe Rogus
**19**
## The Prince of Wales

What a lovely village this is! A collection of old cottages winds up the street to a 15th-century church and, next to that, a magnificent Tudor manor house stands behind a high stone wall. Holcombe Court is not open to the public, but its façade and gardens can be admired from the arched gateway.

The Prince of Wales Inn, situated at the bottom end of the village, is the sort of pub Holcombe Rogus deserves. The 17th-century building has been renovated sympathetically. Inside, all is cosy and traditional without being 'twee'. There are oak beams, walls decorated with stags' heads and horse brasses, and wooden settle furniture. There is one main bar, but other rooms lead off – a cosy family room on one side and a large restaurant on the other. Another section has skittles and darts. Outside is an enclosed beer garden.

A blackboard lists the excellent range of real ales on offer, with such brews as Cotleigh Tawny and Old Buzzard, Otter Bitter and Wadworth 6X, earning the Prince of Wales a regular mention in the *Good Beer Guide*. Dry Blackthorn draught cider and a full range of wines are also available, house wines being on tap. And the food provided is superb too. Daily specials, written on the blackboard, supplement the regular items. There are bar snacks, full meals and an à la carte menu. Salads and sandwiches, steaks and pies, seafood dishes and fish courses, vegetable bakes and pasta meals, curries and grills; the choice is mouth-watering and there is something for everyone.

Normal pub opening times are kept, although the place is closed on Tuesday lunchtimes.

Telephone: 01823 672070.

*How to get there:* Holcombe Rogus stands in the north-east corner of Devon, close to the Somerset border. It lies only 2½ miles off the A38, 8 miles north-east of Tiverton and 6 miles west of Wellington. The M5 (junction 27) is a little further away. The Prince of Wales will be found next to a small garage and petrol station, standing back from the village street.

*Parking:* There is a large pub car park. Vehicles can also be left along the main village street, which is not busy.

*Length of the walk:* 3½ miles (2½ mile shorter option). OS map Landranger 181 Minehead (inn GR 059189).

*This route includes a stretch of towpath, thus offering a walk along one of the few canals in South West England. To reach this canal public footpaths are used, across fields and over stiles. The return is made along a country lane. One short stretch runs through a quarry and walkers are advised to take care. The scenery in this part of Devon is undulating rather than hilly, so there are no steep gradients. The walk along the canalside is especially attractive and the area is a haven to a wealth of wildlife.*

## The Walk

The route begins down the wide gravel track that runs past the western walls of the Prince of Wales and its car park. This takes you through a farmyard and on past some barns. Beyond these continue straight on, along the edges of a number of fields. At first the hedgerow is on your left, then later it is on your right, later still it is on your left again. All the while the trackway is clear, being wide and

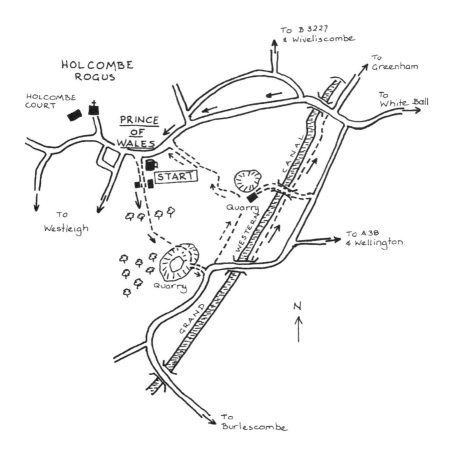

tractor-rutted. Eventually this track ends at a gate, beside which is a stile half-hidden by undergrowth. You will see a yellow arrow painted on the post, pointing the way ahead. Continue over this stile, through a small thicket and then through a gate. Thereafter bear half-left. Ahead you will see a tree-covered hillside. The path, running diagonally across the field, in fact skirts this hill, rising gradually to contour along its lower slope. At the top corner another stile leads you through to the quarry.

The tree-covered hill in fact hides a large sandstone quarry. Having climbed the stile you emerge onto the top edge of this commercial complex, and see close at hand the sad destruction caused by rampant mineral exploitation. The right of way actually goes through this quarry, but since work still continues on weekdays, you may be directed around the left-hand edge. In any case, keep the deepest part of the quarry – the excavated hole – to your right as you follow the gravel track down to the road on the far side. When you meet the road turn left to reach the canal. Upon reaching this waterway you have a choice of routes. You can either shorten the circuit by a mile, or continue with the route as planned. In the former case take the footpath on the left just before the canal, which runs along the western side of the water, and then returns to Holcombe Rogus via the next quarry. If keeping to the main route, drop down to the towpath using the stone steps on the right-hand side of the bridge and then follow the canal north.

The Grand Western Canal, as this waterway is called, is all that remains of a canal that was originally meant to connect the English Channel with the Bristol Channel. This stretch was opened in 1838 and linked Tiverton with Taunton. Sadly, it was never a great success, losing most of its traffic to the railways. It became disused by the 1920s and, by the 1960s, had all but disappeared. The section which runs through Somerset has now, indeed, gone but the Devon section has wisely been restored, thanks to the Tiverton Canal Preservation Society and Devon County Council. The whole stretch is designated as a Country Park and, as such, is back in full use as a tourist attraction. The walk along the towpath is lovely, with tall ash trees creating a green avenue where swans and other wildlife live in happy contentment. Take your time along here and enjoy the solitude. At the far end the towpath climbs to the road where you turn left. The Prince of Wales is little more than ½ mile away.

## Places of interest nearby

The *Grand Western Canal* provides facilities for anglers and boat enthusiasts as well as walkers. At the Tiverton end, horse-drawn narrow boats run a passenger service. Just north of Tiverton is the National Trust property of *Knightshayes Court*, a Victorian Gothic mansion surrounded by formal gardens.

# ⑳ Dunkeswell
## The Royal Oak

High in the Blackdown Hills, the village stands attractively on the edge of Dunkeswell Moor, a plateau which has been used as an airfield since the Second World War. It is a popular spot – and the Royal Oak further adds to its popularity.

There has been an inn here since the 1830s, although the building itself is older, probably dating from medieval times. The character has been well maintained, the interior boasting low ceiling beams, exposed stone walls and a wood-plank floor.

There is one large bar with a pool table at one end and a dining room up some steps at the other end. All is dark and cosy. The former stable block has been converted into a skittle alley and function room. Outside is a large beer garden where peacocks wander around, together with other tamed birds. Barbecues are held in summer and live music is often provided, at special events. Children are very welcome and a family room is available. In short, the Royal Oak is the perfect place where you can eat, drink and relax.

As a freehouse various real ales are offered, including Wadworth

6X and Flowers Original, as well as Scrumpy Jack draught cider, and a varied selection of wines. But it is the food that especially attracts the customers. Apart from the wide-ranging regular menu, daily specials are written up on the blackboards. There are always items suitable for vegetarians and children have their own menu choice. Bar snacks include sandwiches, ploughman's lunches and jacket potatoes. Light meals feature macaroni cheese and things with chips, and the choice of main dishes ranges from steaks and chicken to trout and pies. The sweets include various ice creams, fruit sundaes and treacle tart. The Sunday carvery, in the separate restaurant, is very popular. Normal pub opening times are kept.

Telephone: 01404 891280.

*How to get there:* Dunkeswell lies just 5 miles north of Honiton and 12 miles south-east of Tiverton. It is best approached from the eastern end of the Honiton bypass. The Royal Oak stands at the southern (bottom) end of the village.

*Parking:* There is a large pub car park. Vehicles can also be left along the main village street, provided no obstruction is caused.

*Length of the walk:* 2½ miles. OS map Landranger 192 Exeter and Sidmouth (inn GR 140076).

*This is a lovely, unspoilt corner of Devon where gently sloping wooded valleys dissect a broad, upland mass of Upper Greensand – a rock producing fertile plateau scenery. There are many footpaths all around, also numerous tracks and narrow country lanes. From the nearby summits, Dartmoor and Exmoor can both be seen on the distant horizons. This walk wanders along the valley of the Madford river, an upper tributary of the river Culm. The route is very clear throughout since it employs well marked footpaths and hedged trackways. There are some gradients to negotiate, and a few stiles, but nothing should cause any difficulty.*

**The Walk**
From the Royal Oak walk uphill, taking the second lane on the right in order to reach the church, which stands attractively in a little hollow. Continue round behind the churchyard and turn right along the lane signposted to Dunkeswell Abbey (which is 2 miles away

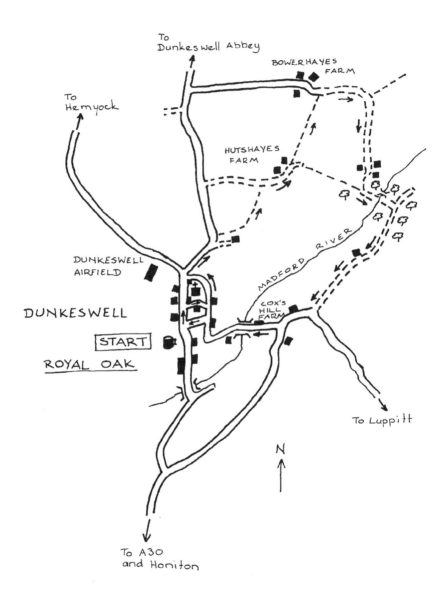

and not included in this walk). This lane climbs fairly steeply and bears left. Almost immediately after this bend, take the footpath signposted off to the right, where a kissing-gate leads you through the hedgerow.

The path is clear so you can concentrate on the scenery. Through the trees, which slope down to your right, you will glimpse the hills beyond Luppitt, the far summit being Dumpdon Hill, where stands an Iron Age hill fort. The river, down in the valley immediately below the path, is the Madford, which flows north. Two miles downstream it passes the site of Dunkeswell Abbey, a monastery founded in the 13th century by Lord Brewer, one of the four men who ruled England while Richard the Lionheart was away fighting the crusades.

A short way along the footpath a second kissing-gate takes you into the field on your left. Continue along the edge of this until you reach a track. Turn right and walk down to Hutshayes Farm. After bending left around the farmhouse this track ends, close by some barns. Go through the gate ahead and continue straight on, in the direction indicated by the arrow sign. Keeping close to the hedgerow (on your left) and admiring the views (to your right) you will soon reach Bowerhayes Farm, on the far side of the second field. There, a stile leads you onto a track, where you turn right.

This rough tarmac trackway is marked as a bridleway and descends fairly steeply into the valley. At the bottom it ends at a small group of cottages and farm buildings, bearing right just before stopping at a gate. Fear not, for the footpath continues and a stile, next to the gate, indicates your way ahead. An earthy path, between hedgebanks, now leads you downhill. Keeping left at the junction (another track joining from the right) you soon reach a ford. Wading across, however, is *not* necessary. A plank bridge, amongst the trees to your left, will carry you across. Take your time here, and notice the remnants of a stone bridge beside the flowing waters. Was this once an old clapper bridge? Maybe not, but certainly this trackway must once have been more important as a routeway than it is today. Perhaps it was part of a valley road to the medieval abbey downstream.

After crossing the Madford river the way back to Dunkeswell is easy. The grassy, rutted track bears right and climbs out of the valley, beneath a line of trees. After a steep ascent the surface becomes firmer with gravel and the track continues south until it meets a country lane. Keep right, walk past Cox's Hill Farm and turn right again. Now, crossing the valley for the second time, you pass various

*Dunkeswell airfield.*

handsome old cottages to reach the main part of the village. Turn left at the village hall and left again to reach the Royal Oak.

## Places of interest nearby

*Dunkeswell Airfield* regularly holds special flying events, aviation exhibitions and sightseeing flights. Refreshments are always available. Near Willand (7 miles west) is the *Verbeer Manor Country Park*, which is ideal for families. Near Uffculme (8 miles north-west) is *Coldharbour Mill*, a working wool museum. The town of *Honiton* is also worth a visit, having numerous antique shops and an interesting lace museum.